"Many talented creatives flop at freelancing because they don't know how to bid on a project, negotiate a contract or manage client expectations. Kristen Fischer is on a mission to ensure you don't become one of them. By the time you're done reading this smart, comprehensive guide, you'll be a lean, mean business machine."

—Michelle Goodman, author of
The Anti 9-to-5 Guide and *My So-Called Freelance Life*

When Talent Isn't Enough

Business Basics for the Creatively Inclined

Kristen Fischer

CAREER PRESS

The Career Press, Inc.
Pompton Plains, NJ

Copyright © 2013 by Kristen Fischer

WHEN TALENT ISN'T ENOUGH
EDITED BY JODI BRANDON
TYPESET BY GINA TALUCCI
Cover design by Ian Shimkoviak/theBookDesigners
Printed in the U.S.A.

To order this title, please call toll-free 1-800-CAREER-1 (NJ and Canada: 201-848-0310) to order using VISA or MasterCard, or for further information on books from Career Press.

The Career Press, Inc.
220 West Parkway, Unit 12
Pompton Plains, NJ 07444
www.careerpress.com

Library of Congress Cataloging-in-Publication Data

Fischer, Kristen.
    When talent isn't enough : business basics for the creatively inclined : for creative
        professionals including artists, writers, designers, bloggers, Web developers, and
        anyone else looking to freelance or run their own business / by Kristen Fischer.
            p. cm.
    Includes index.
    ISBN 978-1-60163-250-0 -- ISBN 978-1-60163-543-3 (ebook)
        1. Arts--Vocational guidance. 2. Arts--Marketing. 3. Self-employed. 4. Small
        business. I. Title.

NX163.F57 2013
658.02'2--dc23
                                                                    2012039162

For Joe Fischer, my father-in-law, who always takes the time to ask me, "How's business?" Your support for my professional endeavors—and this book—means the world to me.

Acknowledgments

Special thanks to my literary agent, Kathleen Rushall, for believing in this project and making it a reality. The team at Marsal Lyon Literary Agency was instrumental in providing both guidance and patience.

Thank you to the team at Career Press for your publishing expertise.

My gratitude goes out to Richard Streitfeld and Kiffanie Stahle for providing valuable wisdom and professional knowledge.

All of the talented people that shared their stories so candidly have helped other creative professionals tremendously.

Thank you to the New England Patriots, who motivate and inspire me.

Norma, thank you so much for being amazing at what you do and being a true light.

Danielle, Ken, Mom and Dad Fischer, and the rest of my family and friends: Your kind words, support, and enthusiasm have empowered me. I am beyond blessed to have each of you in my life—cats included.

Charlotte, Quinnan, and Lyla: You each inspire me to reach higher.

My loving gratitude goes out to my mother. You are the foundation, you are the support, you are my friend.

To my wonderful husband, Tim: Thank you for listening to me, loving me, and making me laugh. You are my one and only. I wouldn't be living happily ever after without you.

And to my Lord, I really can do *all* things through You.

"We must be careful not to exhaust ourselves 'waiting for inspiration' when we could have simply been working."
—Julia Cameron, author, *The Artist's Way*

Contents

Author's Note

All quotations from freelancers, in the text and in the Q&A sections, are the result of personal conversations, either in person or via e-mail, between the subjects and me throughout the course of the last year.

Foreword

As a creative business coach, one of the first questions I ask a new client is, "Why did you decide to go into business for yourself?" Although the answers may vary greatly, usually the core reason is the same for most of my clients: freedom. Some people are needed at home during "normal" working hours, but are still required to contribute to the household income; and some people, like me, find that after years of working for others, they are happiest and most productive when they get to call all their own shots.

No matter what your personal reasons are for starting out in the great adventure that is being self-employed, chances are at some point you're going to need more resources, support, and even encouragement to keep your business strong, and to keep that feeling of freedom. That is where books like this become invaluable resources for people like us.

Although you may have a wonderful education and loads of hands-on experience in your field, chances are when you were a student, intern, employee, assistant, or even a coworker, your experiences were lacking or possibly non-existent in some of the basic skills you need to run a healthy, thriving business. Just because you own your own business doesn't mean you know everything there is to know. It's okay to ask questions, seek out help, and make it up as you go along.

Getting bigger and better clients, marketing yourself, hiring legal help, and working with an accounts person takes practice and a basic working knowledge of what those duties and services are. Seeking support from a book like the one you are now holding in your hands is a great place to start when you simply don't know where to begin or even how to finish.

Kristen has written a wonderful guide to help you decide what will work best for you and your business, while leaving the choices up to you, thus helping you retain that precious freedom.

Good luck and get down to business with your creative self,

Kari Chapin
Best-selling author of the creative business books
The Handmade Marketplace: How to Sell Your Crafts Locally, Globally and Online and *Grow Your Handmade Business: How to Envision, Develop, and Sustain a Successful Creative Business*

Introduction

Chances are that you are a talented person if you've picked up this book. You may be a whiz Web developer who can churn out gorgeous, functional Web sites. Or an illustrator who can bring a drawing to life. Maybe you're a jewelry designer who constructs beautiful necklaces, earrings, and bracelets. Or you may be a writer, like me, with a knack for stringing words together. Whatever your creative talent is, it can be something you enjoy as a hobby—or, as many creative professionals have proved, it can be the source from which you make a living.

Have you ever thought about making a living off your artistic ability? Many people start a creative business—it's relatively simple to launch due to the low overhead costs—but never build the foundation necessary for long-term success. Why? They think all they need is their talent. They do not realize that they need to know how to manage a business, too.

A business doesn't stay strong for too long if you think that you can rely on your flair for prose or eye for design. For example, a competent graphic designer probably can create a logo, but how does he or she secure a client? How can he or she satisfy that client? What happens if the client does not like that first draft? When the project is over, assuming it went well, how does he or she bill for the work? And what about paying taxes on the money earned?

15

To make a living doing what you love, you will need to go beyond simply *doing* what you love. There are other aspects of running an enterprise that you will have to be familiar with—yet not necessarily *master*—in order to excel. You don't have to calculate taxes yourself to keep your business going strong, but you *will* need to understand some financial principles to build and sustain it. On the same note, you may very well be able to work from home in your pajamas, but you will have to have a professional tone when you're on the phone with clients as if you are face-to-face. In short, you will have to *do business* to have a business.

They say, "Do what you love; the money will follow," however, that's not entirely true. The income only follows when you treat your creative venture like a *real* business—because that's what it is! Without some professional know-how, you won't be able to establish a legal entity, attract and retain clients, earn enough money, manage your finances, or protect your rights.

I know, it sounds like everything is about money, money, money. Well, a business operation *is* about money. It is about technicalities. And it can definitely involve things you don't *like* to do. Earning enough money isn't the only measure of success, yet it is a viable component of true professional achievement.

My first book, *Creatively Self-Employed: How Writers and Artists Deal with Career Ups and Downs*, was about coping with the emotions related to leading a creative venture. I didn't really talk about the nuts and bolts of business. At the time, I felt there were plenty of resources that gave the basics. After several years running my own copywriting business, I've learned that there are tools out there to help people start general businesses—but only few cater to creative moonlighters and full-time freelancers. As such, most of them are overwhelming, dry, and difficult to comprehend.

That's why I wrote this book; my hope is that it gives you information that is easy to understand and relate to, and hopefully enjoyable to read.

Whether you go straight to the chapter that entices you most, or you read this book cover to cover, my wish for you is to find the tools you need. I want you to build a strong business that stands the test of time, provides you with a gratifying lifestyle, thrives even during a recession, and, most importantly, lets you enjoy all the wonderful feelings that come with doing something you are innately good at.

Chapter 1

It Takes More Than Talent

I was in the fourth grade when I wrote an essay about my kitten, Tangles. After my teacher, Mr. Wolf, read the piece, he nominated me to attend a young authors' conference at our local community college. Mr. Wolf was the first person to recognize my talent. At the time, I didn't know I had any.

It poked through as I grew, but it wasn't until my sophomore in college when I was studying environmental science when it re-emerged. I heard that the school's homecoming queen was selected via an essay contest and thought it was cool that the school picked royalty based on skill rather than looks. So I applied and, soon after, there I was, wearing a plum velvet gown and a rhinestone crown.

These were just glimpses of the talent that was inside of me—a gift that I never recognized until the crown came off, I had a bachelor's degree, and began working. Upon graduation, I had little desire to save the earth; I knew my heart wasn't in it.

There were some prospects for me to be an environmental scientist, but none caught my eye. On a whim, I decided to apply to be a reporter at a local newspaper and got the job. Now it was my *duty* to write. Seven years later, I am a full-time freelance copywriter and journalist.

I am intrigued by creative professionals. I have connected with solo professionals—or *solo-pros*, as I like to call them—that run the gamut. Some are veterans who freelanced before freelancing was hip, others are rookies off to a thriving start, and others are running a side business while they juggle a traditional full-time job. Most of them are genuinely talented, yet naively believe their artistic ability is all they need to be a business owner.

Some creatives talk more about their natural gifts than they do about delivering for the clients that are paying their bills. Many don't work *with* their clients because they are "the talent"—and think they are somehow above providing customer service or building client relationships. Others can't get out of the "starving artist" mentality and scrape by feeling completely unfulfilled.

There is definitely an important factor in using your talent to live off of, or just to lead a profitable side gig: You need to know how to *run a business*, not just *create*.

I subscribe to the theory that if your creative gift is your profession, you're going to need to be able to *sell* what you produce or provide. That involves being more focused on staying in business and using your natural gifts to do so, and less about hand-picking clients and charging exorbitant rates because anything less would diminish your God-given gifts.

I'm aware there are different measures of success. Some creative professionals may not have to support themselves or their households financially, so whatever kind of creative gig they have is an accomplishment. Really, it doesn't matter how you measure success. If you want a strong business that you enjoy, you need to possess some business awareness. That means building a client base, learning to work with clients that you may not love, filing taxes fairly, and mastering negotiations. It means keeping accurate records and marketing your business. And if you moonlight, it means going beyond "hobby mode," whether you want to keep a side gig or turn it into a full-time career.

When I worked as a reporter, I was able to hone my writing abilities well and efficiently meet the editors' needs. That carried over when I launched my copywriting business; even though most of what I write isn't exactly hard-hitting prose (it is content used to sell products and services), I still know how to gather information and produce material that meets the needs of my clients—and often surpasses them.

My business has expanded to writing books and magazine articles, and I still use my editorial abilities. I love to write, whether it's short, snappy content to sell products or a compelling, witty article in a magazine.

That said, I wouldn't be where I am if I did not embrace professional best practices. My talent, no matter how wonderfully undiscovered and raw it was when I penned those essays earlier in life, wouldn't have helped me create such a fulfilling career if I did not incorporate sound business strategies.

This is the key to long-term success as a creative professional: You have to *do* business and *mean* business to *stay* in business. Your talent is just as important, but it's not the only thing that matters.

What is more important in running a creative business—your talent or your business know-how?

"This is one of those chicken–egg sorts of things. You need the talent to create work people will want but you need business skills to get the work seen and noticed. I have seen a lot of artists with so-so work and really great business skills make way more money than someone who has a lot of talent and no business skills. So business skills are definitely a must if you want to make a living from your work."

—Claudine Hellmuth, illustrator/artist, *www.claudinehellmuth.com*

One can get by on one's talent, but only for so long. Clients don't want to hire the artist that won't incorporate their feedback—otherwise, they won't refer that ever-so-talented artist to their colleagues. People talk in the industry. It does not take long to see that one guy is difficult to work with, and a company can hire someone just as gifted who is willing to work *with* them. The same goes for the administrative end of it: You may be a pro with clients lined up around the block, but if you don't pay taxes on what you have earned, Uncle Sam will come knocking.

Creatives have different priorities for their businesses; one of mine is being able to live a comfortable lifestyle—not to have to work 40 hours a week, every week. To be able to work from where I want, and have my choice of clients. To enjoy the projects I take on and have a steady pipeline of work coming in. Through time, I've been able to make my vision a reality. Every day isn't perfect, nor is every client, but I wouldn't want to be doing anything else with my life. I want you to be able to do the same, no matter what your ambitions entail.

According to the 2012 Freelance Industry Report (available at *www.internationalfreelancersday.com/2012report*), people launch their own creative business for a number of reasons. About 28 percent of freelancers chose to go solo for more freedom and flexibility, 23 percent did so to follow their passion, 13 percent wanted to be their own boss, and 29 percent got into it "accidentally."

Regardless of how they started their own businesses, this chapter will introduce you to some freelancers who appreciate and have developed their talent—and who integrate business principles into their career. This chapter will not discount that your talent is probably amazing; instead, it will give you the tools you need to draw upon it and excel as a creative professional.

Do you think many people let their ego over their talent get in the way of business?

"I tend to see younger and less-experienced creatives get tangled in ego issues. This manifests itself in an unhealthy "us vs. them" mentality. To a degree most creatives have some level of ego, but it's about keeping things in check while still remaining confident. At the end of the day, people don't want to hire and work with jerks no matter how talented they are. Make the interaction about building a partnership and not battling an adversary."

—Jay Rogers, designer/illustrator, *www.jayrodesign.com*

Getting Started: Setting Up Shop...or Studio

One part of launching a creative business that does not involve your artistic ability is deciding to earn money off your talents, whether it is a side business or your primary role.

Von Glitschka (*www.vonglitschka.com*), an illustrative designer from Oregon, has been in business for more than a decade. (You may know him because we hosted the Freelance Radio [*www.freelanceradio.com*] podcast together, along with our moonlighter friend, Dickie Adams. You may also know Glitschka's name because he is an author, teacher, and speaker.)

One of the biggest reasons Glitschka has been so successful is because he took time to learn about business when he began. Just because marketing and client relations were two facets of business that came naturally to him, he was still aware that he needed legal and financial advice because those areas were not his strong suits.

He retained a business lawyer, who explained how tax, payroll, and bookkeeping systems worked. Then one of his clients told him about a small business management program at a local college; he took the course. He says it was extremely intimidating because he is not a math fan, but it helped tremendously.

"I signed up and became friends with the guy that ran it and he mentored me," recalls Glitschka. "He got to know my business, and then audited how I could improve it business wise. That was a big eye opener."

As a result, he decided to hire a bookkeeper and a CPA. Though he isn't glued to a calculator, he knows what records to keep so these professionals can accurately report his earnings. *That's* doing business.

Just as you would with any other venture, it's important to do things properly. In other words, even though you can probably set up your creative business in your spare bedroom (mine only required a computer, technically), that's not necessarily enough. Choosing a business model, devising professional goals, and formulating your internal processes are just as important.

As a result of the strong business platform, Glitschka has been able to build an impressive reputation for himself and garner top-name clients—all while providing for his family financially.

"I know creative people who'd I consider better than me and they are struggling to make ends meet...not because of lack of skill, talent or craft, but due to lack of business sense and operating a business," he says. "Commercial artists may be commercially centric but they can still be starving artists if they don't know business basics."

How can a creative individual decide if he or she should start their own business or just freelance on the side?

"I did it the moonlighting way. I had a day job and I worked really hard at my own business until it was so big I could barely keep up. I got laid off in a company-wide layoff and just at the time my own business was really starting to take over so it was perfect timing. The disadvantage is you have to essentially work two jobs, your real job and the one you are building, but the advantage is you can do it without worrying about money and that takes a lot of pressure off your little fledging business."

—Claudine Hellmuth, illustrator/artist, *www.claudinehellmuth.com*

Why Creating Isn't Enough

Chances are, you realize that you need more than just your artistic side to make your business work. Obviously you will need to engage clients, which involves marketing and selling, too.

Glitschka says that too many creative professionals believe if they simply create, the clients will come, and—*bam!*—they are in business. That's not the case. Your artistic flair can be the greatest thing out there, but you need to be the one marketing yourself so prospects see why you are the best for the project. Otherwise, someone with just as much talent *and* business sense will get those jobs. Let's face it: Someone else can generate deliverables just as lovely as yours, but not all creatives can combine the talent *and* business know-how—and that's what separates flourishing business owners from those who try freelancing and are forced to go back to a 9-to-5 job they dislike.

Stephanie Jones (*www.cleverfinch.com*), a designer from Virginia, worked at numerous advertising agencies in account planning and strategy before delving into the artistic world. This background has been effective in helping her meet her clients' goals. She never had to step off a high horse of "I have my talent and that's all I need," when she started her creative enterprise; she knew business was equally as important from the start.

"I always knew how important it was to be professional with my business, even when it's not focused on the fun part," she says. "Being a strategic resource for your clients builds value, and you don't just build that by creating pretty design pieces."

Finding Your Creative Edge

Glitschka is a natural connector, and leverages this ability to cultivate what I call the *creative edge*. Your creative edge is comprised of the things that set you apart from others when you use your natural abilities. I'm not talking only about your artistic talents; I mean strengths like speaking, listening, writing, coaching, analyzing, mediating, and networking. These aspects, along with your talent and business expertise, can become your competitive advantage.

Glitschka is also involved in the design community. Spending time online communicating with fellow designers and creatives, as well as attending in-person events, has helped him to stand out as a thought leader in the industry. Clients want the "go-to guy" for their campaigns; they want the very best and turn to him for it. This has given him a creative edge.

Why do freelancers need to learn more about business basics?

"While legal and financial advisors can help with things such as incorporation, taxes, contracts, and collections, you still need to know the basics. How much should you charge? When should payment be due? What can you do when a client is late or refuses to pay? Things are continually changing in our industry. So, it's not only important to keep up on current trends and software, but also with changing laws, policies, and more."

—Julie Cortés, co-founder, *www.freelancersu.com*

Customer Service Trumps Talent

Is the customer always right? It's the age-old debate. Although the customer may very well be wrong sometimes, in most cases, they are paying you to do a job that goes beyond using your creative abilities; it involves meeting their needs and expectations, and *that* requires more than your ability to write, paint, or design.

So many creatives are wrapped up in their artistic ability and the way they think a project should go, and do not partner *with* clients. Upon the first inkling of criticism, they insist their artwork is best and refuse to compromise. Ultimately, this can trigger a tense relationship or lead to the end of it—along with the added drama of a check "in the mail" that never arrives. From there, it can become a legal matter—just another reason why you must be business-savvy.

Let's take Alan, a fictional example of a creative who, unlike Glitschka and Jones, didn't see how important it was to concentrate on business and instead focused more on his natural gifts. Alan is a very bright designer with an impeccable artistic eye. So when his client, a major beauty company, hired him to conceive some ads for a new product line, they were shocked to find out that the aesthetic didn't align with their branding platform at all. They had met with Alan to define their objectives, but Alan went with his original concept for the design and never stopped to listen to what the client wanted.

When the client saw the work, which was alluring but not at all in line with their company, they told Alan that they didn't like it and they wanted him to go back to the drawing board.

Alan's problem is that instead of working *with* the client to polish the work, he took all their criticisms to heart (I know, it can be hard *not* to do) and became extremely defensive. He maintained that the design met their needs and then told them that because he was the designer, they should trust his expertise. Oh no, Alan—that attitude will send you right back to a smelly office with fluorescent lighting.

The problem with Alan and creative professionals like him is that even if his design was gorgeous, he never made an effort to satisfy his client. Hopefully when a client hires you, they know what some of your existing work looks or reads like to get a feel for your competencies.

If you don't have the business sense to ask specific questions, you can totally miss the mark and the final product could be way off-target, as Alan's was. And if you don't build a revision process into your contract, you may hit the client with fees that extend past their budget—likely ticking them off even more. You can spend all the time in the world producing the "best" material, but if a client doesn't like it—and you don't know how to cope with that—you can lose the client along with your credibility as a professional. You have to be able to work together, even if you are the one who is open to feedback and the client is the one on the defensive side of things.

Why's that, you may ask? Think about corporate America. If a company used an in-house designer, they would have pulled that person into the conference room and ripped apart the design (politely, I'd hope), and then that designer would have gone back to his or her desk, grunted a little, and fixed the problem. Ultimately, the client would have gotten what they wanted. This is why I think so many companies fear working with contractors; they don't want to put a great deal of money into a project fearing it will come back all wrong. If you want to work with larger companies, you have to be prepared to understand the concepts of customer service. You have to be able to gratify them, even if you hate the final design.

This doesn't mean the customer is always right or that you can't give your professional opinion; it means you have to build your business to accommodate their needs, from the way you express your business practices and word your contract to the communication techniques you use.

How can solo-pros be more attentive to customer service?

"I think that being in any kind of creative services industry is a delicate dance between leading the client and following the client. I think it's a constant back and forth, so I lead for a while, then you lead for a while...and at the end of the day, the client gets to lead, meaning the client gets to determine the ultimate direction of the project because they're the one putting the money into the project. You are a client service and that means that they get to call the shots."

—Todd Henry, founder/CEO, *www.accidentalcreative.com*

Aligning Your Work With the Client's Vision

Delivering positive customer service is obviously a big part of operating a business, but it goes beyond just being nice or spending that five extra minutes on the phone with a client in a pinch. If you know what your role is as a freelancer and strive to understand the client well, you will better grasp the vision of the project, which can help prevent sticky situations and result in more clients singing your praise.

Todd Henry, who founded the creative consulting firm Accidental Creative (*www.accidentalcreative.com*), believes that solo-pros need to take time to understand what their clients want in order to satisfy them.

As much as I think I understand what a client wants sometimes, I, too, have had situations when the customer isn't happy with what I have produced. In that case, I have learned to take a "How can we improve this?" stance rather than the "Why don't you like my work?" or "There must be something wrong with me!" approach.

When our work doesn't match up to the client's vision, we have to be willing to "let go of our pride and our ego," says Henry, who hails from Cincinatti. Otherwise, you could have an unsatisfied client on your hands that won't use your services again or, even worse, tell others not to.

Letting the client know that the project is a collaborative process from the start is vital. That way, even if it's not exactly what the client wanted, you can still team up to make it just right. Otherwise, they may not be open to revising the deliverable if needed, and insist that you did not do what they asked. During client consultations, I almost always let the client know about the revision process—namely, that I build a few rounds of revisions into the cost. Not only is it a selling point because it provides peace of mind that they won't be stuck with something they don't like; it lets the client know not to judge the first draft too harshly because I am available to help them make it sparkle.

Must-Read
The Accidental Creative: How to Be Brilliant at a Moment's Notice
by Todd Henry

Taming Your Inner Critic

Sometimes the clients aren't the harsh ones—we are. This is another issue that can cause roadblocks if you want to run a strong creative business.

In the beginning of my copywriting career, I was the one who demanded perfection more than my clients. If my first attempt wasn't flawless, I would be furious with myself. I knew revising was important, but I wanted every client to be picture-perfect happy with what I did. When they were not so pleased or suggested changes, I would go hard on myself and tell myself that I was wrong. Sure, sometimes I would be defensive and have to "take five" to calm myself down, but mostly I was completely too critical and harsh on myself. I didn't know at the time that in not educating the client about the creative process, or believing in it myself, I was making work much more stressful than it needed to be.

So the work had to be edited—so what? Once I really understood revisions were necessary—and a great way to improve customer service—I put the concept into my sales pitch, started getting excited about pleasing clients, and received more positive feedback and referrals for going the extra mile to satisfy customers.

Not all clients will be pleased with what you do, no matter how many times you try to tweak the deliverable. When the client demands perfection out of the first draft or first stab at a concept, you have to reassure them that it is all right to refine it. This is the part of the project when you start to put your ego aside even if what they want is off the wall. Again, in educating a client up front that revisions are often necessary, you are less likely to have an irate client—and if you've had one, you'll do anything to prevent it from happening again. Client relations is a big aspect of being business-savvy; it's *not* just all about how to file taxes!

Are We All Egomaniacs?

George Coghill (*www.coghillcartooning.com*), a cartoon logo artist and designer from Ohio, believes solo-pros identify themselves as artists, so when criticism comes their way, it's natural to take it personally.

That's why it's important to realize that you are creating for *someone else*—not yourself. What you produce is subjective—some people will like it and others won't—but if someone else is footing the bill for it, you have to heed their input.

"I think the successful artists are able to tame the ego," Coghill notes. "It's tough to take direction on your creativity, and if you let it get to you it can hurt."

Jones admits that she relied more on her talent than her business acumen in the beginning. "I slowly learned more about how to defend my work and fine-tune my creative brief so I was coming closer to achieving the client's goals and my own," she explains. "Slowly shifting from relying solely on my talent to relying on my talent *and* business skills."

Fusing Talent and Professionalism

What Jones has done is use her talent *along with her business skills*—a recipe for success.

"You don't like the first draft of that brochure, dear client? What would you like to change? Let's talk about it." (Client relations.) "I do think you should keep this section because I believe it will be a help to accomplish your marketing goals." (Negotiation.) "Okay, how do these changes work for you? Let me know what else I can do to help." (Customer service.) "Your total is on this invoice. Thanks for your business!" (Accounting.) These are all pieces of business that are separate from your artistic talent yet must be incorporated if you want to flourish.

Once you embrace that you need to deliver customer service, and that being self-employed isn't all about you, you'll have a happier base of clients and peace of mind. Doing what you love will be enjoyable—as it should be.

Must-Read
Breaking into Freelance Illustration: A Guide for Artists, Designers and Illustrators by **Holly DeWolf**

Money Matters

Another reason that some creatives focus more on their craft than they do on business is because they do not believe money is important. And I realize that, because the majority of us choose to use our gifts because we're truly happy when we create. I'm not out to make millions; I just want to make enough to live on and do what ignites my creative spirit.

But starving artists are a thing of the past. You don't have to be poor to practice your creative talent. Plenty of copywriters I know make upward of six figures a year and I know artists that pull in enough to support their entire families on one income.

Perhaps most of us just want "enough to get by" because we think that's all we're worth, but that's not true. Though you may not want to charge top-dollar as a rookie solo-pro, you can still charge—and earn—a competitive wage.

Some charge too much, some too little—and others don't know what the heck they're making. When I interviewed Jones, she said she knew plenty of designers working all day who think they are making hoards of money, but don't know how much they earn. "They think they're making money, but really they're not. And it's even more concerning that they're clueless about it," Jones notes.

When I think about freelancers and money, some main concepts come up: Creative professionals charge either too low or too high, don't pay or properly complete taxes, and do not put the legal means in place to ensure they get paid. We are going to talk about all of these aspects in the coming chapters.

What types of financial goals should I set when launching a creative business?

"Initially to be able to at least come close to breaking even. Within a year or so to be making as much or more than working for someone else. If you can't meet these goals realistically, the attractions of working for yourself versus working for someone else have to be very, very strong, or done out of necessity. Pay particular attention to your

billable efficiency—i.e., the percentage of available hours that are actually billed to clients. Service businesses that average under 50 percent billable efficiency are seldom successful."

—Cameron Foote, principal/editor, *www.creativebusiness.com*

Henry believes that it is difficult for freelancers to think in terms of money or want to deal with numbers because it is a challenge to turn their thoughts into value, or to value their contributions.

"The tendency is to underestimate the value you are bringing to the process," he advises.

He says we emphasize our artistic nature instead of incorporating business principles because we tend to be more into creative *ideas*, not necessarily *outcomes*.

Think about it: Did you or are you thinking of starting your business primarily to make money? No, that's secondary. The primary goal is to be able to do what you love, right? It was for me, too.

In that respect, it's understandable that you are more focused on your talent when you start out. Perhaps you want to deliver good customer service and satisfy clients, so you focus solely on your talent, or what you can deliver. Who cares about a contract, right? You just want to be able to create a logo for this really cool coffee company, or draft an annual report for a big-name national vendor. Once you hear a few positive remarks about your work, it can feel tremendously rewarding. Then you think, "Hmm, maybe I am good at this. Maybe I can really do this! Maybe I really am a writer/photographer/designer/blogger."

Look, there's nothing wrong with appreciating your talent—or centering your energy on it. Once the honeymoon is over, however, you may realize that not all projects give you butterflies. That's when you're going to have to be very efficient with your time, and time is money.

This is really the ultimate goal, isn't it? Not to spend half your day compiling invoices and the other half creating, but to get the business practices down pat so you can spend more time doing what you love.

It's reasonable that you want to do what excites you; few people are brave enough to even entertain the idea of trying to make a business based on their talent. You will just have to make an effort to put as much into the business aspects as you will with the creative time. In time, maybe even the "business ickies" will be enjoyable for you, or at least they won't take up too much time. (Hey, invoicing could sort of be fun if you think about all the money coming in—especially if you took the time to ink a contract and ensure you'll actually get paid.) If not, you will have to simply accept that business practices have to be a part—but not all—of what you do as a creative professional.

Must-Read
Creative, Inc.: The Ultimate Guide to Running a Successful Freelance Business **by Joy Deangdeelert Cho and Meg Mateo Ilasco**

Make Business Part of Your Business

Elise Cripe knows how important revenue is. The blogger uses her Web site (*www.eliseblaha.typepad.com*) to promote her workshops and the sale of her paper goods, and also earns income from advertisements on the site. I frequent her blog a lot for visual inspiration and have always been impressed at how she ties her talents into making a living. Though she is artistic, she also puts a great deal of emphasis on being professional.

"I like to say that it doesn't matter how smart or creative you are. If you can't communicate your idea or market it well, it will never bring profits or rewards," says the California-based blogger. "I think talent gets you started, but business know-how will keep you going."

Cripe says it is vital to keep track of money. "Don't underestimate the importance of tracking the money," she says. "Save everything and keep notes on expenses. If numbers are not your thing, then consider hiring someone to handle that aspect of your business." (See? You don't have to be a QuickBooks whiz or understand what Section 179 of the Internal Revenue Code is.)

Cripe says her genuine love of writing helped her blog to grow into a revenue-generator. Although blogging is part of her full-time job, she says it is not the only way she brings in money. "I wear many different hats to generate my total income, but blogging is the glue that holds it all together," adds Cripe, who draws a small amount of income from sidebar advertisements and affiliate program commissions. Her blog evolved into a vehicle to promote on-line workshops she teaches on paper crafting and Web design, and is also the on-line shop where she sells charming paper goods.

The blog has opened up numerous opportunities for her as well, as Cripe has secured consulting gigs and product design projects.

"All have been very unique experiences and something I am so grateful for," she adds. "I have been blessed to turn my hobbies into something that generates income for my family."

What skills must creative professionals possess innately—and which can be learned?

"The only innate 'skill' I believe one needs is a passion for what you are doing. Creativity and business can be learned through focused practice/repetition. One needs an overabundance of passion for what they are doing to keep them going through the inevitable rough business periods. If you aren't in it completely, it will be very easy to be discouraged and the business will eventually suffer."

—George Coghill, cartoon logo artist/designer,
www.coghillcartooning.com

A Little About Me

Before we get going on all of the juicy details that will help you run an awesome biz, I want you to know my story. It may help you better understand where I came from, why I felt the need to write this book—and why you may want to take some of the advice in it.

After graduating college and securing my first two jobs as a newspaper reporter, I then switched gears and entered the environmental industry. I knew I loved writing, so when a job came up for a technical writer at an environmental company that offered better pay, I took it. The chance to do some corporate writing (and the ability to alleviate my fears about not "using" my environmental studies degree) was all I needed to move into a less-creative sector. I worked there for about two years when I realized how much I had loved writing and journalism—just not necessarily the job I was in at the time.

About that time, I began exploring creative careers and I guess you could say stumbled upon the concept of copywriting. I never knew that it existed, or that it could be a lucrative career. At the time, I had a boss who would pick apart my highly technical environmental reports, which did little for my self-esteem. Soon after I discovered copywriting, I inquired about taking on some projects for a local two-woman creative firm. I remember being so nervous to meet the women at a local coffeehouse that I didn't even offer to pay for our drinks before I left. I was so thrilled that they thought my writing was promising. "What a ditz I am," I thought when I realized I forgot to offer to pick up the tab. "They'll never hire me."

But they did, and I was amazed. From there, I started moonlighting. About a year later, I wanted to take my business to the next level and be out on my own, but I knew I wasn't quite ready financially. Most of my hesitation was because full-time freelancing didn't offer steady pay, and without a traditional job it would be tough to get health insurance, which my momma said never to go without. What was the next logical step?

I applied for a part-time job as a copy editor at a bigger newspaper. It required evening hours so I could develop my copywriting business during the day. Finally, I had a solution I felt good about: I wasn't taking an all-out plunge into full-time freelancing, but I was on the right path. I could build up my business, earn a steady paycheck, and dive into full-time freelancing once I knew my business was sustainable.

No job is perfect, though (even the ones you cherry-pick). At the newspaper, all of the copy editors except for the veterans had to travel to the warehouse about 20 minutes away once a week to proofread pages as they came off the printer. The problem was that I was going nearly every night I worked. The warehouse didn't exactly feel like a safe place—particularly at 1 a.m.—and I soon got fed up being the boss in my freelance life and being treated like a peasant at my part-time gig.

After about a year as an editor in the doldrums of a warehouse instead of a newsroom, my copywriting business was booming. I was engaged to be married to my husband, Tim, and I would soon be able to go under his medical insurance—a monumental relief.

I connected with a prospective client who wanted to hire me part-time and let me work from home—score! Now I could transition to working from home full-time, but still have a steady income coming in from a stable job.

It all sounded great until I left the newspaper and the new job fell through. "Now, I'm screwed," I thought to myself. With nothing else to do but try to find another part-time gig, I started working full-time for myself while I sought another part-time job in the writing field. There I was, doing what I wanted to do. I was a full-time freelancer. I was an *accidental* full-time freelancer.

I never returned on-site as a part-time employee. Things just took off from there. These days, I work mostly from home, primarily because I can. I still take on copywriting projects, but I also have been able to use my journalism expertise to write books and magazine articles. Luckily for me, all of my experiences before becoming a solo-pro were not a waste: I use my technical background and journalism expertise every day. I've built up my skills in the marketing field. Each step I took was helpful to build my talent and business know-how.

For me, baby steps were the only thing that worked, but I know plenty of solo-pros that have taken the plunge headfirst. There is no one right way. To have a creative business, you just have to set yourself up for success and do the best you can, integrating your talent and business knowledge. If you're not sure what you have to offer on the business side of things, you have definitely picked up the right book.

Rock What You've Got

Whether you fall into self-employment without a penny in your pocket or intend to moonlight on the side while you work a full-time job, you have two things to work with: your talent and your ability to do business. Your talent is there already. I'm sure of it!

Your ability to conduct business? That's where I come in. Once you can fuse your gifts and your professionalism, you will be able to thrive. It is my hope that however your creative career plays out, you will be able to enjoy what you do for a living. And if it's in your PJs every day, well, there's nothing wrong with that!

Sweet Success
Diversify and Nurture Your Talent

Few people can make food look appetizing in photos. Kitty Florido (*www.asterisco-sa.com*), a graphic designer and photographer that splits her time between New York and Guatemala, has become pretty good at it. Florido launched her business 12 years ago after she enrolled in some marketing courses. After taking a job in sales for a postcard company, she realized she enjoyed the creative aspects of the job more than the sales part. "I started playing around with design software, and realized I was good at it," she recalls. A few months later she landed her first client, and soon after launched her own business.

When a client needed photographs of food, she started exploring her photography aptitude. Since then, she has completed a class on food photography and recently started a culinary Web site (*www.the-foodieskitchen.com*). She says that her skills as a designer have changed, and a huge part of her business has evolved into the food photography arena—a niche she loves.

Florido says it's important to keep cultivating talent so you have something new to offer clients. For her, developing her natural gifts has been, well, appetizing.

Beginner Mishap
Business Comes First

After Tim Wasson (*www.tjdub.com*), a Web designer from Illinois, graduated from art school, he worked as an illustrator and animator at an advertising agency.

"I just hated having to come to work at a designated time, all the meetings, the time-tracking. I was a creative, damn it!" he recalls. "I detested estimating time on projects, logging hours, answering phone calls, and revising work." That along with being confined to a cubicle was unbearable for Wasson, who was just 21 at the time. He quit the job to pursue life as a solo-pro.

"I assumed my pure talent and portfolio would sell me [as a freelancer], no problem," he says. "What I didn't have, unfortunately, was any skill at all in selling those features to potential clients."

The jobs he did get as a freelancer involved more than just conceptualizing mockups. He had to meet deadlines and keep within project budgets—two things he loathed. "I always fell back to the excuse that 'I'm a creative! I should be able to do what I want...business should be plentiful,'" says Wasson.

He continued to miss deadlines, struggled with client communications, and was puzzled on what to charge for projects.

"My business was crashing and burning," he adds. "I still had a great portfolio, but without the almighty referrals that drive my business today, and with no testimonials, I was going nowhere."

Soon after, he went back to a traditional job. He took another stab at freelancing after a few years, and, though he did better that time around, he eventually took an offer for an in-house design job. Wasson says that running his own business isn't quite for him.

"To be successful, you have to master sales, proposals, and client relations," he notes. "Talent comes after all that."

Chapter 2

It Starts With Your Vision

By now you have figured out that you can't simply say, "I'm in business," to be in business. You need to think strategically about your creative endeavor. In other words, you need to do some business planning.

Part of coordinating your business can be quite fun and allow you to integrate your creative gifts. For example, I was eager to write content for my Web site; when it came time to assemble a payment system, not so much.

This chapter is devoted to a few general aspects of business planning. Parts of it may be exciting, whereas others will make you wish you were watching Snooki drunk-dialing on an episode of *Jersey Shore*. Remember: We're taking the good with the not-so-great here—the "good" being your talent and the "bad" being all the things about running a business that make you cringe. Some parts will appeal; others won't. Do it all anyway. You'll need to spend your time involved in things you don't necessarily like, but you can do it. In the end, it will make your creative business stronger and you'll be better for it.

Welcome to Your Identity Crisis: Selecting a Business Model

Establishing the type of business you will have is often a starting point. Choosing your setup will affect everything, so it is important to select something that works for *you*.

The most common forms of business for self-employed professionals and freelancers are:

→ Sole proprietorship.

→ Limited liability company (LLC).

→ Partnership.

→ Corporation.

→ S corporation.

In my case, I am a sole proprietor because it offers the simplest structure and least tax hassle. Although it does not provide all of the legal protection I would have if I were an LLC, for example, I am comfortable with this model. From the start, I knew I never wanted to expand or form an agency, so this has worked as a long-term solution. Consider what you want to come from your business in the future during the start-up phase when you choose the model.

Karen Larson (*www.lmstudio.com*), a graphic designer and brand strategist from Michigan, started off as a sole proprietor, then formed a partnership. About 15 years ago, she and her business partner took on a huge client project and decided to hire subcontractors.

"Someone in the client's accounting department started making waves about the fact that 'a freelancer' was making so much money, not having a clue about the projects we were working on," she recalls. To avoid having an issue in the future, she said the pair decided to incorporate. "Appearing as a larger entity, this has never been a problem since."

This is a good example of choosing a business model based on what works for *you*. Each model has benefits and disadvantages, so you'll have to select one that is right depending on your individual situation. If you need to consult a lawyer or accountant, it may be a good investment; or you can connect with other freelancers for insight.

Resource
Visit *www.irs.gov* to learn about forming your business.

Which business entities, if any, require the use of a lawyer?

"An attorney will help you do three things: (1) select the right entity type; (2) set the entity up properly; and (3) help plan for problems. Can you do this without a lawyer? Maybe. However, if you don't set up the entity properly you could lose the protection you thought you were gaining. Attorneys can help you talk through possible problems and set in place solutions to those problems before they happen, so that if there is a disagreement, you'll already have a system in place to deal with it."

—Kiffanie Stahle, lawyer, *www.stahlelaw.com*

What's in a Name?

Before you officially form the business and find a kick-butt dot-com Web site address, you want to make sure to name it appropriately. I never wanted to grow into an agency, so using my name was fine for me. If you think you may add a team member or employees in the future, you may want to give it a different name that doesn't identify it as one person. Still, even some of the biggest brands use the lead creative in their names—take Diane von Furstenberg or Tommy Hilfiger.

You will also want to do a search of trade names (if you are in the United States, you can visit your state's Secretary of State Web site) to see if the name is already in use. You then may also want to see what domain names are available. Nothing stinks more than having a phenomenal name but having to sacrifice it for a difficult-to-read URL. So do some research and whittle it down to a few choices, then make your selection.

What business aspects are important to include in planning?

"Marketing! Devising a plan to pursue the kind of business you want, the kind of clients you want, and how you will get them so you don't have to take everything that comes along. You need a plan for how you will present yourself and your business to those carefully chosen prospects. It's also important to realize that once you get moving, things will change. Nothing is set in stone.... For everything else, surround yourself with a network of other creative professionals. From there, you will have resources for just about anything you'll need."

—Ilise Benun, author/marketing consultant,
www.marketing-mentor.com

What's Your Personal Brand?

Throughout the book, you are going to learn more about generating client leads and marketing yourself, but I wanted to touch on branding in this chapter, particularly, because it's something you need to think about when you are in the conceptual stages of planning your biz.

Branding is not managing your reputation or advertising. Instead, it draws upon components of communication to give people an idea of what you're all about and what to expect when working with you. It's not about logos, though the visuals on your business cards and Web site are a key aspect of branding. It's really more about the client's experience. You want to use your brand—logos, content development, publicity, and the like—to build credibility, convey a message, and encourage loyalty. You want prospects and clients to want *you and only you*, as if another creative professional will never measure up.

When I think about branding, Bethenny Frankel comes to mind. She's an entrepreneur behind the Skinnygirl alcoholic drinks; many of you may know her from her time on *The Apprentice, Martha Stewart, The Real Housewives of New York*, or *Bethenny Ever After*. Even if you are not a fan of these shows or her, I think you can learn a lot from how this woman created a business—and cultivated an empire.

Now, Frankel is creative, but she is not a creative professional like you or me. Though she set out alone, she now has a large company; she can hire people like you and me to be creative *for* her. From her delicious, low-cal Skinnygirl cocktails and nutrition bars to exercise DVDs and shapewear, they all have two things in common: Her sassy personality is fused into each, as well as her goal to make healthy living achievable for everyone.

Even though most solo-pros may never have that large of a range of products or services, you can still incorporate the same branding principles she used into your business. In Frankel's case, she is all about healthy living, and to me that's her "umbrella" for her nutrition, fitness, and wellness products. Another part of her brand is how she outreaches—through reality shows, speaking engagements, and books. Most people appreciate her honest approach and therefore buy her products because they like her, along with her attitudes on wellness.

In the same sense, you could create an umbrella. I am a copywriter, but I am also a journalist, editor, proofreader, and author. Those are different services in my brand umbrella, but that umbrella also includes the values I bring to work that others do not. The brand is also part of my image.

When a client uses my services, I want them to love working with me so much that they turn to me for every future job—and tell their colleagues, too. I want them to think of me for positive values; in my case that's being a good writer, easy to work with, and affordable. I integrate customer service to retain and satisfy the client. That keeps them coming back to me. *Me*—not anyone else. As a solo-pro, you are your own brand.

Who are you, what do you have to offer, and how can you build trust with potential and current customers? Maybe they have read your blog for months before hiring you; in doing that, you've fostered a connection and established yourself as a dependable professional through effective branding. The customer hires you—and hopefully tells others about you—based on that loyalty, which came from establishing and consistently promoting your brand. *That's* brand success.

You can express your brand and engage people with it even if they are not clients. In fact, plenty of my customers have hired me after "following" me for a while or seeing some of my work elsewhere.

I established my brand and *they came to me* because they wanted *me*, specifically, to work on their campaign.

To start branding, think about who you are. What aspects of your personality shine through to your services? Maybe you really think outside the box. Perhaps you have a whimsical design aesthetic that stands out. Maybe the tone of your writing is punchy and distinctive. Or you consider yourself to have more of a classic flair that seems to have eroded as time has gone by, so you offer a hard-to-find traditional approach. What do you want people to count on you for? These are all things to consider when thinking about your brand. Let me show you more about how I put together mine.

Branding Is About Loyalty—Not Just Looks

I have always considered my brand to be based around the concepts of *straightforward* and *affordable* copywriting services. When clients come to me for help with their writing, I make it as easy as possible. Everything is upfront so they can see what you get. Visit my Web site, for example. The design is simple yet distinctive. The tagline is direct: "Your words are worth a lot. Mine only cost a little." In the content, I detail my business processes. I show samples so prospects can see the type of work I can deliver—solid copy, not fluff. My writing style is equally simplistic for the most part, as well.

Not only do my uncomplicated Web site and logo tie things together to create the visual aspect of my brand, my no-nonsense approach is evident throughout everything I do as a copywriter. On the Freelance Radio podcast, I'm known for my practical tips, along with a blunt, sometimes-sarcastic, and humorous approach to freelancing. Heck, even this book is part of my individual brand because I'm going to be quite direct as I tell you about life as a self-employed creative professional. I want people that need a copywriter to choose me because they know they will get quality work and not pay hundreds of dollars an hour to do so. And I want them to be *loyal*. (Oh, I also want them to tell their friends and colleagues about me, too. Tall order, right?)

That's the goal of branding—to create something that only you can offer and drive prospects to buy in to it.

In the same sense, Frankel wants to be the source you turn to when you think about staying healthy. Because people tend to like her personality, or at least admire her sense of humor and candid nature, they typically want whatever she puts out. (I've purchased one of her books, adore her cocktails, and gave her yoga DVD a shot.) She's not the only brand I turn to for health and fitness products, but I consider her a good source for them.

Apple, for example, has become a trusted brand for many of us. I'm a huge fan of music, so when it comes time to purchase a new digital music device, I'm only going to be looking at iPods because I like the product. In fact, I will still buy another iPod even though my first one gave me the "sad Mac" indicating it was out of service sooner than I thought it should have been. My brand loyalty is to Apple, but even though they make computers, I am still an IBM girl. Knowing that, however, I will only use Dell and HP products because I have had a positive experience with those brands in the past. That's the loyalty that good branding creates. Still, people have to use the product or service and be satisfied with it to keep coming back. That's where customer service comes in.

As a creative professional, you either create products or services. Whatever you produce, make sure everything stays *consistent* and *authentic.* In all you do, think about whether or not it aligns with your brand.

Dan Schawbel (*www.personalbrandingblog.com*), a personal branding guru from Massachusetts, says traditional branding methods include business cards and resumes, whereas nontraditional tools include your LinkedIn profile or blog. Together, they can work powerfully to show the world who you are as a creative individual—and why clients just have to have *you* on their next project.

Branding isn't just creating a logo and slapping it on your Web site and business card; it's about thinking who you want to be and exuding it in all you do. It's all part of that umbrella—what you create, the values that you emulate, how you represent your brand, and your brand's visual appearance.

When Sara Robbins-Page, a jewelry designer from Maryland, launched her line, Heavens to Bessie, she found that marketing her jewelry as "handcrafted" wasn't exactly turning heads because there are so many jewelry designers out there. When she would tell others she was a jewelry designer, she knew they were trying to envision her work and discern how it was different.

If you visit her Web site (*www.heavenstobessie.com*), you can tell off the bat that she has a flair for intricate, personalized designs that are neither too elegant nor eccentric.

"My work focuses on words. Funny quotes, random thoughts, and shouts of devotion have all made my work what it is," explains Robbins-Page, as many of her charms are personalized, often with lively phrases. "The truth is, I sell wit more so than jewelry but my marketing was not so specific."

A client had told her that she did not view her creations as jewelry, but more so as a means to make people smile and express positive messages. That's when Robbins-Page gave herself a branding makeover.

"I began to really market what my work means versus what it actually is," Robbins-Page explains. "This changed what kind of ads I did, where I marketed, and broadened who I marketed to."

The branding and marketing alteration made a huge difference in her business, and she says orders have increased as a result of the revamp.

Why Your Web Site Counts

Part of the reason why Robbins-Page has been so fruitful is because her Web site rocks at conveying her brand. I think the days are over when freelancers can run a thriving business without one. You're going to need to generate leads, showcase clips, describe your work practices, and enable prospects to reach you. Even if you don't know how to design or create a Web site, that's no excuse to skip having one.

Start by nabbing a knockout domain name that goes with your branding strategy. The majority of solo-pros use their name (I do at *www.kristenfischer.com*) but others use other designations, such as the name of their studio. Calvin Lee, a designer from Los Angeles, uses two that redirect to the same page (*www.calvinleedesign.com* and *www. mayhemstudios.com*). A solid design is crucial, so if you are not talented in Web site design, hire someone to help.

Next, you must select a Web site host. Then it is time to build the site. Use a little foresight to think about what you want to create now *and* as your business grows. Maybe you intend to add a client page to list your clients once you acquire more, or you want to eventually build a blog on to the site. Keep those things in mind as you construct your Web site.

It should include the basics: a homepage with an overview of what you offer, a page with details about your services, a biography, a portfolio, and a contact page. You may also want to consider pages on testimonials or a page dedicated to explaining how you conduct business.

Your Web site doesn't have to be super-fancy, either. Something somewhat plain will do so long as it is functional, the links work, and it does not contain typos.

Business Plan or Plan Business?

So here we are with a chapter on business planning, and you're probably going to be shocked to hear that I never created a business plan. Though I do not discount that having a formal business plan can be a valuable tool, it's not imperative for solo-pros. Business plans are more of a necessity when you are looking to raise capital, form a partnership, or expand your business in the long run.

That is not to say that a business plan can't be valuable. Should you choose to draft a business plan, make sure to think of it as a strategic roadmap that not only includes market research and details on competitors, but also sets goals for the future. A business plan can also include operating procedures, financial details by month and quarter, licenses, and tax details.

 Resource
Visit *www.sba.gov* for details on drafting a business plan.

Although I am not a huge advocate of formal business plans, *planning* for your business is vital.

I like to approach business planning the freelancer-friendly way. That is, I don't want it to be daunting or overly complex. Enough aspects of launching a business are intimidating; the planning, at least, should be somewhat exciting! You have the chance to decide what works for you, because it's *your* business and no one else's.

Business Blueprinting

Instead of business planning, I like to use the term *business blue-printing*. To use this technique, I recommend that you think about the following questions objectively and be as honest as possible in your answers. Instead of giving you an outline, I like this approach because it helps you think things through without a constricting formula to follow.

Perhaps you jot down your blueprint in a notebook; that's fine. Or you go heavy into graphics and come up with some color-coded montage of goals; go for it. Just write something down, or at the very least *think* about these things. The questions will help you contemplate all aspects of running a business so you are well-equipped to deal with whatever comes your way.

Keep in mind that it's never too late to create a business blueprint. Additionally, I advise that you review your business blueprint regularly so it evolves as you do.

1. General Goals

    → If you are just beginning, what is the overall objective of your business?

    → If you could change one thing about your business, what would it be and how can you make that shift?

    → Would you consider going back to full-time work or moonlighting for the right opportunity?

    → Do you ideally want to moonlight for the long-term or eventually be self-employed?

    → How will you approach professional development, client relations, administrative tasks, and customer service?

    → What do you want a typical day to be like?

→ How do you envision your business in the next year, three years, five years, or 10 years?

→ How can you better develop your talent?

→ Are there any ways to make more passive income related to what you do?

→ Do you want to be a thought leader in your field or simply work?

→ Who are your creative role models?

2. Marketing Goals

→ What values and services make up your brand? What is your branding goal?

→ What kinds of tools do you think would help you execute or improve your marketing?

→ What types of marketing tools will you use to get clients? Retain clients?

→ Which marketing strategy comes easiest to you? What marketing strategy will not work for you?

→ How will you obtain referrals?

→ What does your Web site need to make it better? Any new sections to add?

3. Financial Goals

→ How much do you want to make per year? What do you need to do in order to achieve that objective?

→ What kinds of returns are you getting on your investments?

→ How can you optimize spending?

→ Do you need to create or revisit a pricing platform? Are you charging competitively for your skill level and geographic area?

→ Will you charge hourly or by project fee? Will you require a deposit? When will invoices be due? What methods will you use to collect payments? How will you respond to late payments?

→ How will you monitor bookkeeping, invoices, and payments?

→ Will you hire a tax professional or do taxes yourself? Do you need to pay quarterly taxes? What kinds of deductions will you take? What receipts and documents must you keep?

4. Legal Goals

→ What type of business model will you/do you use? If you are already in business, do you need to switch the model?

→ What do you think of your contract? Has anyone else reviewed it? If you are already in business, is your contract missing any clauses that you find may come in handy? (Most freelancers create their own contract and have a client sign it. I advise that even if your clients have their own contracts, which you can use, it's good to have your own.)

→ Do you need to hire a lawyer for anything?

5. Client Goals

→ Who is your ideal client? What types of clients would you like to reach?

→ Would you rather have a few regular clients or a larger quantity of clients?

→ Do you want larger projects or shorter gigs? Do you prefer long-term projects?

→ Do you have a specialty area or niche?

→ Will you work on-site, take temporary contracts for part- or full-time work, or hold any part-time/steady gigs?

→ Are there any clients you want to end relationships with? If so, how will you approach them?

6. Administrative Goals

→ What kinds of administrative tools do you need in place?

→ What types of improvements can you execute to make things easier on yourself so you can focus more on the aspects of business you enjoy?

→ What is the ideal office setup that you will work best in?

 Must-Read
The Right-Brain Business Plan: A Creative, Visual Map for Success **by Jennifer Lee**

When you write out or really think about your goals, you are more likely to make them a reality. Some people need to create action steps and assign time lines to each. Feel free to do that. However in-depth you draw out your business planning, make sure to do it in some way, shape, or form. Throughout the rest of the book, we will touch on several of the aspects in this business blueprint, so you'll want to revisit it later.

What Are You Worth?

Let's take a look at some numbers so you can see how other freelancers are charging clients. According to the 2012 Freelance Industry Report published by International Freelancers Academy (*www.internationalfreelancersacademy.com*), 60 percent of freelancers quoted and charged flat project fees, 35 percent billed by the hour, 4 percent used retainers, and just 2 percent utilized other performance-based models.

The report says that 49 percent of freelancers earned anywhere from $20 to $59 per hour (up from 45 percent in 2011) and 33 percent earn more than $70 an hour (down from 36 percent in 2011). These figures lumped together wages from designers, marketing consultants, writers, editors, and the like.

Take a look at some more hourly rates for solo-pros:

- → 11.7 percent made $20 to $29 an hour.
- → 12.2 percent earned $30 and $39 per hour.
- → 10.3 percent made $40 to $49 an hour.
- → 15 percent earned $50 to $59 per hour.
- → 8.2 percent made $60 to $69 an hour.
- → 10.5 percent earned $70 to 79 per hour.
- → 4.1 percent made $80 to $89 an hour.
- → 4.1 percent earned $90 to $99 per hour.

It goes on from there, with some escalations and dips, but it's interesting to notice that 10.6 percent of those surveyed report bringing in $100 to $150 an hour; 2 percent report earnings from $151 to $200 an hour, and another 2 percent say they earn more than $200 hourly.

The survey found that 17.7 percent of Web developers earn $40 to $49 an hour, 18.7 percent of copywriters made $50 to $59 an hour, and 17.2 percent of designers earned $70 to $79 per hour. Check out the report (*www.internationalfreelancersacademy.com*) to learn more about your specific field. The results are interesting and can give you some perspective when putting together your prices.

Let's focus on copywriters' rates so I can illustrate a point. According to the aforementioned report, 5.8 percent of copywriters make between $20 and $29 an hour, 5 percent make from $30 to $39 hourly, 6.5 percent earn from $40 to $49 per hour, and 18.7 percent of copywriters make $50 to $59 an hour. The number of copywriters that earned from $70 to $79 an hour was 16.5 percent in 2012, whereas 17.3 percent said they made $100 to $150 an hour. On the high end, 2.9 percent earned from $151 to $200 hourly, and 3.6 percent made more than $200 an hour.

I like looking at numbers, but basing your rates on these can leave you confused because data differs depending on the source. PayScale, for instance, states that copywriters only get up to $75 an hour when they have at least 20 years of experience under their belt. A *Writer's Digest* guide dubbed "How Much Should I Charge?" breaks down project fees and hourly rates according to different types of writing. It says advertising copywriters can earn anywhere from $35 to $150 an hour.

This is why I don't believe in following just one guide when setting your rates. Look at those figures; they are all over the map! According to them, I could make anywhere from $10 to $200 an hour. Rookie solo-pros may wonder, "How on earth should I charge?" while those with more experience say, "Can I give myself a raise yet? If so, how much should I increase it?"

 Must-Read
The Designer's Guide to Marketing and Pricing: How to Win Clients and What to Charge Them by Ilise Benun and Peleg Top

Hourly Rates vs. Project Fees

Whether you work on an hourly rate, a project fee, or use a mix of both, it is a good idea to have what I call a *baseline hourly rate* to help you establish those rates. The baseline isn't your hourly rate, per se; it's a starting point to base your pricing on.

Your baseline hourly rate will probably differ from your hourly rate because you may not necessarily advertise it; it's just the lowest rate you can make an hour so you always know you wind up having enough to cover your butt—and your taxes. You can probably figure it out after you devise your hourly rate.

Here's a common tactic to figure out your hourly rate: Formulate how much you want to earn taking into account your skill level, geographical region, and other applicable factors. Keep in mind that you will need to pay for taxes and probably health insurance, too. Account for your administrative time, too—that is, the time it takes you to prepare a contract, process a deposit, and invoice for the job. Look at your living costs and other expenses, and any overhead. See what you need to make not only to break even. As you gain more experience, you can always raise your rate.

Next, guesstimate your billable hours, which may be anywhere from 1,000 to 2,000 hours per year, depending on how much you want to work. For example, if you earn $50 an hour and estimate to have 1,000 billable hours, you would earn $50,000 a year. Keep in mind that if you want to earn $50,000 a year, you actually need to pull in much more, because approximately 30 percent of it will go toward taxes. In that case, you'll need to charge more than $50 an hour to make $50 an hour or you could just charge $50 knowing you actually make less.

Now that you have an hourly rate, here's why you probably won't use that in most cases. First off, many clients will want a project fee so they can work it into their budget (otherwise, you can feasibly charge for as many hours as you want). When I charge an hourly fee, I try to give the client a cap—or maximum of hours I will use—so they can work my costs into their budget.

Here's why most freelancers stick to flat fees. Let's say a project pays $2,000 and you estimate it will take 40 hours to complete it; in that case, you've made $50 an hour. What would happen if it took you 45 hours to finish, though? Now you are only making about $44 an hour. Without an extra cushion, your hourly rate goes down. If you finished that same project in 35 hours, now you are earning $57 an hour. That's not too shabby if you want to earn $50 an hour, because you have some extra money to play with, but if you haven't accounted for taxes in that hourly rate, you're going to wind up making much less.

In order to devise project fees, you do need to have some sort of hourly rate to go by. Then you can build in extra fees to cover other factors such as taxes, the time it may take to revise the work, or that ever-important "hassle fee." Of course, some projects will run over, and others will run under what you expect. In time and over time, you will be able to adjust your pricing so you consistently earn or exceed your hourly rate.

Susan Johnston (*www.susan-johnston.com*), a freelance writer in Massachusetts, says she uses both flat fees and hourly fees depending on the scope of work. Some freelancers have different rates depending on the task performed; some clients prefer one billing method over another.

"If a project is clearly defined then a flat fee can work, but if I sense there'll be a lot of back and forth or potential scope creep, an hourly rate ensures that my pay scales according to the time required to get the job done," she notes. "However hourly rates don't reward efficiency the way a flat rate does."

Amy Philip (*www.careercertain.com*), a leadership career consultant from Brooklyn, doesn't believe in hourly fees when you are a creative service delivering a product to a client, but she works mostly with individuals so she can elect to use this method.

"Clients want to know up front what the final cost will be and are not interested in how long it will take to complete the work," she says. "While I do calculate the numbers of hours I anticipate it taking on my end to complete a project to determine my fee structure, I always provide my clients with a flat-rate quote."

She once asked a writer to create a marketing piece for her and was told it would cost $120 per hour. So she asked the next logical question: How many hours will it take?

When the writer said she would not know until she got into it, Philip was puzzled.

"I thought this was really odd and said to myself, 'I'm not interested in how long it's going to take her; I just want to know up front what it's going to cost me,'" she recalls. "From a client perspective, I was only interested in the end product and what the total fee would be. It could take her an hour or 10 to do the work, but that wasn't my concern."

After the experience, it's easy to see why Philip isn't drinking the hourly rate Kool-Aid—and you can probably understand why!

How Do You Charge, Kristen?

I don't drink the hourly rate Kool-Aid much, either; I use mostly flat fees. I advertise that my copywriting rates *start* at $35 an hour to give clients an idea of what I charge. Clients in the marketing arena know the going rates copywriters make for the most part, but clients in other industries typically do not.

My starting hourly rate is on the low- to mid-end of pricing for copy-writers, but I typically earn anywhere from $50 to $100 an hour, and I have earned up to $200 an hour. How do I do it? Am I the queen of deceit?

That $35 an hour is my *advertised starting hourly rate* (not my base-line rate). I often use that rate as a foundation into my pricing, then add more for other factors.

Most copywriters may balk at earning $35 an hour, but that rate is what enables me to attract a wide range of clients. Let me explain.

Let's say that a prospect approaches me to write a Web site. They may be really put off if I said I charge $100—or even $50—an hour. My advertised hourly rate lets them see that I am more on the affordable side of the fence but indicates not to contact me if they can't offer *at least* that much. When I quote my hourly rate or a project fee to a cli-ent, I base it on what I feel is appropriate for a specific project. I may very well start at $35 for some, but I can go higher because $35 was only the *starting* point. This gives me tons of flexibility.

A client doesn't need to know what I make an hour. If they agree to the project fee I devised, then it's a win-win because I won't go over the fee (or their budget). If I work efficiently, I can make a great hourly rate well over my baseline rate *and* hourly rate—and they'll never know. So long as they receive what I promised, it's all good.

When I put together a quote, I try to guesstimate how many hours the work will take me, including factors like geographic area, timing, research, and experience. I always build some time for miscellaneous things that could come up, such as a "quick call to touch base."

Talent and Experience Affect Pricing

In *The Designer's Guide to Marketing and Pricing: How to Win Clients and What to Charge Them*, authors Ilise Benun and Peleg Top bring to light an important factor. The same project that would have taken you 20 hours when you started freelancing may only take, say, 10 hours just a few years later. If you're charging the same hourly fee 10 years after you start, you may earn less because you put in fewer hours. That's why raising your fees can be useful. But it's more than that, according to Benun and Top.

They say that when devising fees, you are selling your years of expertise, the effort you have put into developing your talents, and your consulting acumen. You are also selling peace of mind to clients that they will receive what they want based on your track record. Therefore, the price encompasses timing, but also takes into consideration your location, project urgency, how much you need the work, and even what they call the "aggravation factor." Include costs for any on-site travel, and I always take into account the client. (A startup will likely have less to pay.) All of that should be built into your hourly rate, or your project fee. Though you have to cover other costs to account for these factors in your fee, it's a tough balance because you don't want to penalize the client with a higher rate just to cover things like taxes, benefits, and administrative costs.

Resource
Visit *www.freelanceswitch.com/rates* for an hourly rate calculator.

When should you accept a job that pays lower than what you would like?

"Sometimes you have to bite the bullet on price if there's some other payoff. For example, I'll take on an assignment for a reduced fee if I really want a particular company on my client roster but they can't pay my standard rate, or if the finished project would enhance my portfolio. I also think it's important to lend my expertise to charities, so I'll occasionally donate my work or offer lower rates to these organizations. Be discerning about how many of these 'freebie' projects you take on, though, because you can easily find yourself overcommitted to non- or low-paying work. Know when to say no!"

—Lisa McComsey, writer/editor/marketing consultant,
www.lisamccomsey.com

What Are You Worth?

Coming up with a price is a big challenge for just about every creative business owner I know. You want something competitive, but you also want to be able to attract enough clients to keep money coming in. You probably know what is too low for you, but what is too high? What's just right?

I advise freelancers to do their research and come up with a starting point, then go up from there. Know your baseline rate and use it to formulate lump-sum fees. If you advertise one rate as a rookie, you can always change it in the future; you are entitled to.

Philip advises to think about where you want to position yourself in the market: Do you want to be on the low end, marketing yourself as a value player? Do you want to be in the middle, or do you want to be a premium service provider and charge on the higher end?

"Pricing in many ways dictates how you will be perceived by clients. I have found that people believe that you get what you pay for," she adds.

Negotiating Your Rate

One of the nicest things about being your own boss is being able to negotiate your rate. Everything is negotiable; don't be offended too much if a client asks you to come down a bit, but do know that you have the power to negotiate just as much as a client.

Philip says she never negotiates her fee structure; doing so devalues her services and products and is not fair to clients who paid the full rate. Most of her projects take a similar amount of time based on the individual service, so that works for her.

What happens when you provide a wide range of services and the projects can go from small to massive? For instance, I have clients that contact me for an hour of editing and also have clients that have month-long projects that require 12-hour days. In both cases, I charge differently. Although I don't negotiate my rate to a point where I don't make out financially, I have lowered it when I thought it would be to my benefit. For example, I'll give a break to a client who can guarantee more large-scale projects that will give me a chunk of money to bank for leaner months over negotiating my rate with a smaller project. Why? Smaller projects tend to take more time administratively to process. I will also consider taking less than what I want if the work is regular, or if it is for a client whose name will look fantastic on my client list.

When you set your rate, make sure you go high enough so that if you decide to come down in price, you are still making enough money to turn a profit on the project. Nothing stinks more than realizing you are making below your baseline rate after a "successful" negotiation. I always leave a little wiggle room in my fee or rate for a client who wants to bargain, but I always make sure that I never go below that baseline rate or fee—no matter how nice someone is or what he or she promises.

Keep in mind what I just said: You can *choose* to negotiate or not to. Certainly, there is nothing wrong with letting a client know that you will not adjust your rate, but do expect some clients will want to see if they can score the best deal. They can easily find another freelancer who can do just as good of a job for a little less. It's a tight rope to walk—your desire to secure gigs while earning enough to turn a profit.

One more thing when it comes to pricing: You can charge on the higher end of fees, earning upward of or more than the $100-an-hour mark like some of the creatives mentioned earlier in those statistics I rattled off. As a solo-pro, however, you may not be working an average 40-hour week. You may work more, but not all of those hours are *billable*. If you price things too high, especially if you are not a seasoned pro, you may not receive the quantity of projects to make ends meet.

Freelancing can be very lucrative once you get the hang of it, so if you are just starting out remember that you don't always have to charge the rate you earn now. There is this little-known treat called giving yourself a raise, which we'll discuss next.

It's Payday, Baby: Giving Yourself a Raise

Every time someone asks me for my hourly rate, I think about how far I have come because it used to be quite paltry.

It took me a while to become comfortable with fees I charge. As you build your skills and have more to offer clients, it is inevitable to consider upping your fees. I read more often than not that freelancers do not charge enough, and that's true; some don't. Heck, many colleagues would say that I still don't charge enough. Still, I find that more freelancers *overprice* their services because they try to charge what a report says they should make or what seasoned pros earn.

That said, it is natural to want to increase your pay from time to time. How do you know when it's time for a boost? You have to give it time and constantly re-evaluate. If most clients aren't trying to talk you down on a regular basis, they likely find your pricing appropriate. The goal is not to make your prices so high that you're always negotiating; it's to stay on top of what's competitive in your field, geographical area, and all those other factors mentioned earlier. Gradually, over time, you may find it only makes sense to boost your rates; you may find what you made isn't really covering your expenses or skill level well enough.

Raising your rate doesn't require a big public relations campaign or anything; just raise them and update any collateral with the change. In fact, you may grandfather the rate in for existing clients that you really enjoy working for if they will not be able to afford the increase. Eventually, you will get to a rate you feel good about.

How do you know if you're charging too little?

"A good client will tell you when your price is too low and insist that you raise it. Otherwise, you may suspect that's the case when the prospect accepts your proposed price immediately, almost as if they want to lock it in before you change your mind and raise it. But the best way to know for sure is to ask selected peers and colleagues how much they charge, and the best technique is by offering up that information first. They will often reciprocate."

—Ilise Benun, author/marketing consultant,
www.marketing-mentor.com

Promoting Your Rate

Once you have an idea of how much you will charge, should you tell everyone about it? That's a common debate among freelancers. Some say that giving your rate or a range "weeds out" low-balling clients. On the other side, freelancers advocate keeping rates private so they can explain, one-on-one, the value that goes into pricing.

Some solo-pros do not advertise their rates; naturally so, because rates may fluctuate depending on a variety of factors including different services. If you put your rates online, you may feel locked into that amount, which leaves you little wiggle room should you need or want to bill more.

You can also give a fee or rate range, though personally I think that is difficult because all projects are different. Still, a range gives a prospect some idea of where you stand.

Finally, you can give your starting rate, which can obviously go higher depending on various aspects related to the project. This is what I have chosen to do, because it tells low-ballers that I am not interested. It doesn't lock me in to any one fee, but it does give clients a ballpark. In my case, I would rather not spend the time trying to talk a low-baller prospect into my rate or fee because that's a waste of time.

You don't have to promote your fees, your rates, or even a range. You can simply have clients contact you directly about pricing. Being able to choose how you do or do not promote your fees is part of the beauty of having your own creative business—and this is one area where you have complete control.

There is *no one "right" answer* or one-size-fits-all solution to the issue of establishing or promoting your costs. The good news is that you can always change your mind not only about what you charge, but how you tell the world about it.

Quotes and Estimates

When a client asks for a quote or estimate, I never give a price off the bat. Instead, I take time to learn more about the project then crunch some numbers before putting together the quote or estimate in writing. A quote or estimate is just that—an assessed fee for services. Sometimes you only need a quote or estimate for simple jobs, but you probably want to go further and include a little bit about the scope of work involved for a larger gig.

In that case, creating a proposal is a solid way to take the time to think your quote through and tailor your pitch to meet the client's needs.

A Note on Proposals

From time to time, you may have to give a prospective client more than a quote or estimate, so it's a good idea to learn about proposals. A proposal consists of more than just a financial estimate; it contains specifics about how you will approach the job and what the scope of work entails.

Clients often need written proposals for their records or for budgeting purposes, and it's good to have everything in writing so you can avoid *scope creep*, a term coined for when a client tries to get more than you originally agreed to.

Depending on the type of proposal you create, it could require minimal work or a chunk of time.

"Writing proposals is very time-consuming," says Benun, who also created The Proposal Bundle, an in-depth resource on proposals. (Visit *www.proposalbundle.com* and *www.marketing-mentor-toolbox.com* to check out some of her very useful resources.)

Benun says that proposals take time to prepare, so it's a good idea to make sure the prospect has enough money for your services. (Another reason to promote a fee and rate range!)

"Make sure the prospect can afford you in the first place," Benun says. "That usually means talking about money early on—a good habit to get into no matter what."

By the time you get through the proposal process, you should have already had multiple communications with your prospect, addressing all the important issues and asking all the right questions, she advises. The proposal is essentially a detailed confirmation, recap, or expansion of what's been discussed, including the project's budget.

Pick Your Proposal: The 4 Types of Proposals

Benun notes that there are four general types of proposal to choose from depending on the scope of the project and your familiarity with the prospect or client. Keep in mind that most clients will not pay you to put together a proposal.

1. One-Page Agreement

I use this format most commonly. It's not really much of a proposal, aside for the fact that I write out a short (maybe one or two-line) scope of work. It is best used for small projects and/or projects for an ongoing client. It should take very little time to generate; just form a template and plug in the details. I put mine on letterhead so it looks professional. **Time:** 15 minutes or less.

2. Short Proposal (1–3 Pages)

The structure of a short proposal is similar to that of the one-pager and almost as minimal. It's ideal for a new prospect that's already sold but wants the details of what you'll do in writing. Like the one-page agreement, it outlines project basics but adds more detail such as the amount of concepts delivered or words per page. Benun recommends it if your prospect has not worked with a creative freelancer before. **Time:** One hour or less.

3. Medium Proposal (4–10 Pages)

Benun says that this proposal is ideal for a medium to large project for either a prospect or an existing client who will be selling you up the chain to others who don't know you. This proposal typically requires more pages because the client has higher expectations, Benun notes. Again, you can create a template, then "plug and play" some of the details to save time, but you will have to write a little. **Time:** No more than four hours.

4. Long Proposal (10–20+ Pages)

For a major project with Ideal Client Inc., the long proposal is an important marketing tool. "As a general rule, the higher your fee, the more pages your proposal will need to have. A longer document provides substance and shows that you've thought through the project and know what you're talking about," Benun says. Include lots of relevant examples and figures that will reflect on you as an expert, so you can show that you have the experience and knowledge for the project. **Time:** One to two days.

Must-Read
The Fire Starter Sessions: A Soulful + Practical Guide to Creating Success on Your Own Terms **by Danielle LaPorte**

Writing a Project-Winning Proposal

Writing can be overwhelming even for some wordsmiths, so Benun recommends an in-person meeting or phone call for bigger jobs.

Benun suggests asking these questions in order to create a proposal that will get you the job.

1. What are the big-picture goals of this project?
2. What is the specific objective you need to achieve?
3. How will you measure the success of this project?
4. What/who is the market for this product or service?
5. Who is the main decision-maker on this project?
6. What models are you using for this project?
7. Where is the source content coming from?
8. How much research will be necessary?
9. Are there specific technologies you do or do not want used?
10. How does this project fit into your big picture?
11. Have you ever done something like this before? If so, what?

Also, be sure to find out when the prospect expects the proposal so you can deliver it in a timely manner. From there, you will hopefully win the job and can start working on it.

Show Off Your Sizzle With a Portfolio

When you go into business for yourself, assembling a portfolio can help you showcase your work in order to boost credibility and ultimately land more clients. This valuable must-have defines you and your talents. Whether it includes photos of your crafts, clips of your articles, or samples of print marketing collateral you designed, what goes into your portfolio matters—big time.

As a beginner, you will strive to populate your portfolio with samples of your work, but as time goes on, you may find yourself being more selective about what goes in the portfolio because you want it to represent your very best work. Sometimes you love something until a client changes it, and then you may not want to include it. This is your call.

The goal of a strong portfolio is threefold: You want it to highlight the range of services you offer, show off your capabilities, and resonate with the prospect so they will hire you.

For a writer like myself, I want to show that I can handle print collateral such as brochures and also craft press releases, blog posts, and newsletter articles. My portfolio has a blend of projects to highlight my diverse capabilities. When a prospect sees it, I want him or her to think, "Wow, this piece of collateral looks great—I think she can do the same for me!"

You can have either a printed, tangible portfolio to bring with you on meetings (an iPad is a nice touch if you have one), or a section on your Web site for samples. Like many solo-pros, I use both. My handheld portfolio, a leather-bound book with scrapbook-like pages, holds press releases, magazine articles, and brochures. As a newbie, I used it a lot because I would travel much more on-site to meet with prospects; nowadays, I don't have as many meetings so I rely on my Web site portfolio.

Depending on what you do, you can organize your portfolio into different sections. Mine goes by the type of collateral to show prospects the breadth of my experience. You may want to structure the portfolio by industries you have worked in so you can show your expertise in different arenas.

One challenge in creating a portfolio is that some clients do not want their work in your portfolio. This is not entirely uncommon for freelancers. I typically let clients choose if I can use their project in my portfolio; most say yes. A few agencies, however, have had me sign off that I cannot use the collateral—or state that I have worked for the client, because it is really *their* client. Some agencies and firms inflict this rule so their client doesn't see their work was "farmed" out to a contractor. Sometimes, not being able to show off the work you did—or even name the client you worked for—is a complete bummer, but it can be part of the business.

If you are concerned about not being able to put project collateral in your portfolio, talk to a client directly; perhaps if you cannot use the collateral you have created, you can still state you have worked with their brand name. It may sound like listing brands or companies you have worked with is a bit shallow, but prospects and existing clients like to hear their contractor can win over the big guys and identify with companies they have heard of. Again, your image is everything when you're a solo-pro, so you need to make that an important aspect of your business planning.

How can moonlighters best manage their time between their creative business and their 9-to-5 jobs?

"Working 40+ hours per week for an employer while adding your own business to your plate is certainly a challenge. Without much time for charging your batteries, it is a recipe for creative burn-out. I won't lie; I did call in sick from my day-job a couple of times to make myself available for client meetings or projects for my own freelance business. I even brought a USB key to my day-job a handful of times when it was slow and plugged away on freelance projects there (who was to know unless my boss wandered around the corner?). Basically, I learned that if I wanted to be my own boss eventually, I'd have to make the sacrifice of my own personal time for a while. It's a busy transition and leaves very little free time, but it worked out in the end."

—Angela Ferraro-Fanning, graphic designer, *www.1331design.com*

Barter or Trade—or Not

It seems that the concept of bartering, or trading services, comes up for a lot of rookies and those that work with start-ups. This occurs when both parties agree to swap services and waive the fees so it's an even trade. Doing this offers a cost-effective way to receive the services you need.

For example, if you are starting out as a writer or blogger and need a Web site, you might contact a Web site designer and offer to write the content for his site if he creates your Web site. It can get tricky, however, when one party does not need the service right away, or if a service is worth more money than the one being traded.

You can also barter or trade services with clients—that would have nothing to do with obtaining a service you need to start your business. In that case, a writer would provide writing services in exchange for a client's service. If your client was a spa, that may be a great idea because a free massage or two is pretty useful; on the other hand, if your client was a podiatrist and your feet are perfect, you wouldn't need his services—so the barter would be a bust.

Use your judgment to see if bartering is a smooth move, or if doing so will require you to trade in your sanity instead. It is definitely something to consider when you look at all the services you may need to set up a business.

The Help

In addition to swapping services, you can always hire outside professionals to take care of the things you don't like to or cannot do. There is nothing wrong hiring a bookkeeper, for example, to handle your records. Realizing your weaknesses (or tasks that you'd rather not give too much attention to) helps you to focus on parts of business that let you use your talent.

Accounting is a facet of business that Robbins-Page said she knew she needed help with from the start. She proceeded to interview an accountant when she was forming her business, and pays the accountant a retainer to answer questions along the way. Hiring professionals with complementary services not only frees up her time to create; it gives her credible advice she can count on. This expertise is worth every penny for Robbins-Page, who says she has turned higher profits as a result.

In the next two chapters, we're going to delve into a few of those areas that I think the majority of us detest a little (or a lot): legal matters, accounting, bookkeeping, health benefits, and retirement planning. When you hold a traditional job, the company handles these things, but as a solo-pro you will need to have a basic understanding of them. If you choose to hire a lawyer or accountant that's perfectly all right, but you still need to be familiar with these matters because they impact your business and reflect upon you—personally *and* professionally.

I promise, I will make it as painless as possible. Don't pass these next chapters by. Start stepping up like the pro you are and get on the road to running a profitable, legitimate, and fulfilling business you can feel good about.

Sweet Success
A Fishy Offer?

Jay Rogers, a designer and illustrator from Georgia (*www. jayrodesign.com*), says he was once paid for a project in fish. Yes, real scaly fish.

When Rogers was in school, a classmate who was also a fisherman, was studying wildlife illustration. He asked Rogers to help design business cards and offered to pay him—in fish. Mahi, to be exact.

Never one to turn down fresh fish, Rogers took on the project and the whole thing worked out well.

"It was probably the most delicious of the designs I've done in my career," he jokes.

In this case, it was the perfect bartering deal—even though it may have sounded fishy at first!

Beginner Mishap
A Gem of a Business Plan

When Sara Robbins-Page, a jewelry designer from Baltimore, wanted to expand her jewelry-making side gig into a full-on creative business, she didn't think the transition would be too hard.

"I would just continue to create jewelry, only now I would make more of it," recalls Robbins-Page, whose line is dubbed Heavens to Bessie (*www.heavenstobessie.com*).

Ironically enough, she knew how to create a business plan but didn't think she would need it since she already had a taste of what it was like to run her operation.

"I couldn't have been more wrong," she admits. "Without a clear plan, I really had nothing to focus on in between orders."

After working for a while without a strategy, Robbins-Page decided to draft a formal business plan. "I am the sort of person who has a list and a plan for when I go to the grocery store, but somehow I thought I could make my business grow without one," she adds.

Ever since she drafted the plan, it has worked wonders for her.

"Every day I have things that need to be accomplished. There are none of those spaces in between orders where I sit and twiddle my thumbs," she notes.

Every few months, Robbins-Page reviews the plan to get a better idea of what she has accomplished and what she will do next. Her story highlights the importance of good planning—whether it is formal in writing or not!

Chapter 3

Lessons in Legalese

You may wince upon hearing the words *legal, law,* and *contract,* but by now you should understand that a legitimate business involves being familiar with legal matters. Have the right legal resources and measures in place, and you will be able to protect yourself while you do what you love. Skip the legal mumbo jumbo, and you could be dealing with some major ramifications.

Taking charge of legal issues does not mean that you have to spend thousands of dollars to hire a lawyer; it means that you remain aware of what situations you may face and you take proactive steps to stay protected. Yes, you might have to hire a lawyer along the way depending on different situations you run into; that's a *good* thing, because lawyers offer solid information you can count on.

After you establish your business, the "legal stuff" isn't over. Using a contract is a vital aspect to guarantee a well-functioning, professional, and protected business—and then you must enforce it. Not only does a contract help you define the scope of work for a project (and have it in writing to refer back to should the client "scope creep"), it ensures you are protected if the client wants to terminate the project early or chooses not to pay up. These are very common occurrences in the free-lance world, so you need to safeguard yourself in writing, *every* time. Yes, kids, think of it as safe sex for creative professionals: Always use protection.

How much does it cost to work with a lawyer, and what can I expect from the process?

"The attorney may work with you on either an hourly, flat fee, contingency, or pro bono basis. Typically working with an attorney will start with an initial consultation where you will discuss the problem you are facing and the attorney may outline your legal options. These consultations can be free or you could be charged. If you are charged, you may get a credit for the cost of the consultation on your first bill. At the end of the consultation, the lawyer will indicate if they are capable and willing to work on your problem and if so, the terms of your relationship. It then becomes your decision to decide if you want to work with this lawyer."

—Kiffanie Stahle, lawyer, *www.stahlelaw.com*

Do I Need a Lawyer?

This chapter will give you an overview of basic legal matters that apply to freelancers. Even though I was apprehensive putting it together because I do not possess in-depth knowledge in the field, I knew it was necessary because freelancers cannot let themselves be taken advantage of. Simply put, you must protect yourself and your interests.

Sure, a lawyer may make more an hour than you may ever bill an hour, but these well-informed professionals can provide peace of mind *and* protection. That said, I know plenty of solo-pros that have never used use a lawyer. It really depends on the situation at hand; if you use a Web site such as *www.legalzoom.com*, you may never have to meet an attorney.

Consider using a lawyer if you:

→   Want advice on choosing a business model.

→   Need help drafting a contract.

→ Are sued by a client.

→ Are audited by the IRS.

→ Are considering adding a partner or expanding your business.

If you do need a lawyer, you will be best off with a business lawyer, intellectual property lawyer (also known as a copyright lawyer), or contract lawyer.

Resource
Visit *www.findlaw.com*, *www.avvo.com*, **or** *www.lawyers.com* **to connect with legal professionals in your area. State Lawyers for the Arts groups can put you in touch with lawyers that usually work with creative professionals.**

Getting It in Writing: Using Contracts

A contract is a must-have for every freelancer, whether you sign a contract from a client or you provide your own for the client to sign.

I've heard stories from solo-pros that think they are above using a contract, and I always wonder how that mindset is possible. A contract not only gives you the foundation to specify the project scope, it offers a platform so you can enforce receiving compensation for your time.

Actually, I use my contract as a selling point when I am talking with a prospect. I let the potential client know that the contract guarantees they receive the project on time and that I provide any revisions needed.

Now, you may be able to get away without having a contract if you make products and sell them, such as crafts or artwork. In that case, you just sell goods to a customer, but the minute a customer becomes a client who resells your work or carries your crafts in their store, or you license your work, you're going to need a written agreement.

Take it from Penelope Dullaghan (*www.penelopedullaghan.com*), an illustrator from North Carolina. During her first year as a freelance illustrator, she didn't think she needed a contract. "I just expected clients to call me for jobs, e-mail me perfect specs so I could do the job, and they'd send the money in full as soon as they saw my invoice. Done deal," Dullaghan remembers.

She began working for a client who she had spoken with over the phone, and asked for a $500 deposit to start the project. The client paid the deposit right away and liked the first draft. Dullaghan went on to make a few tweaks, thinking the task was nearly finished.

The client then sent her an e-mail saying the scope of work had changed, and wanted her to redo the design at no extra charge.

"I managed to squeak out that I was a bit unhappy about the project changing so drastically, but I proceeded to redo it anyway. That was the nice thing to do," she says. She pitched a second idea and says she thought the client was happy with it.

That was until another e-mail came, informing her that the scope had changed again, and the client wanted to sever ties. The client indicated they wanted their deposit back because they were not bound by a contract—and they would *sue* if she didn't cooperate.

"I was stunned. I had no idea something like this could happen. I wanted to quit my job and slink back to my 9-to-5 day job of steady paychecks and contract-free living," Dullaghan recalls. "I cried for three days straight."

In the end, she refunded the money and moved on, vowing never to put herself in that situation again. It was hard, because Dullaghan is a very trustworthy person—but when you get burned, you obviously learn these kinds of lessons the hard way.

This story exemplifies the reason why it is imperative to have a standard contract in place. You can either draft one yourself or turn to a legal professional for assistance. Even if a client has their own contract, it's still a good idea to have your own so you are at the ready when you get a bite for a project.

Option #1: Hiring a Lawyer to Create Your Contract

Although you certainly do not need to hire a lawyer to create your written agreement, it can be a worthwhile investment. If you choose to go this route, find a lawyer that not only understands contracts but intellectual property, especially if you are an artist, designer, or crafter.

Ed Gandia (*www.edgandia.com*), a copywriter from Georgia, decided to hire an attorney to draft his standard contract. "I think that the biggest reason to use a written agreement is not as much for legal reasons as it is for avoiding finger-pointing," he says. "It's tough to argue against you if you can clearly defend your position with an agreement the client read and signed."

Gandia suggests having an attorney draft a standard agreement that includes all protections plus any other specifications the attorney recommends. His attorney created a contract that lets him change the scope of work and pricing specifications depending on the project. He says it cost about $1,000 to draft the agreement, but he has used it well more than 100 times, so it more than paid for itself.

Check with a lawyer about pricing before you craft the contract so you know the costs up front. Ask the lawyer if he or she has a standard contract to start from so the contract does not have to be written from scratch, which can save time. Some lawyers offer a flat fee for this sort of thing.

Resource
Visit *www.legalmatch.com*, *www.findlaw.com*, **or** *www.lawyers.com* **to search for lawyers in your area.**

Option #2: Building Your Own Contract

You may be thinking, "How on earth can I write a legal contract for myself when I'm not even sure how to put together content for my Web site?" That's a completely understandable question. However, I am pretty confident that you'll be able to form an agreement with a little effort.

These are some components in a basic contract, which you can adopt into your own document.

→ **Add a document title.** Title the document "Work for Hire Agreement" or "Independent Contractor Agreement."

→ **Identify both parties.** The first paragraph of the contract typically states that you and the client agree to terms of the contract, and includes both of your full names and addresses.

→ **Note the date.** That first paragraph also includes the date on which you entered into the agreement. The contract can also stipulate when the terms of the agreement expire.

→ **Describe the Scope of Work.** In this section, you detail what the work involves. I know freelancers that spell it out, and I also know some that say the contract refers to terms as specified via e-mail, phone call, or appendix. Best bet? Spell it out. If I am writing a Web site, for example, I usually specify which pages are included. Just as important is to specify what is *not* included.

→ **Say who owns what.** Detail who owns the rights to the work.

→ **Note who provides materials.** Generally, you will provide the materials to produce the work, but sometimes you need materials from the clients. For instance, I typically use old brochures and Web site content to help me develop new collateral, so specifying that the client is responsible for background material is a good idea.

→ **Talk about payment.** A section on the payment should detail the amount you will be paid, the form of payment accepted, when the payment is due, and if any deposit is due (plus when the balance from a deposit is due.) Also, add a section to specify if late or rush fees will be charged. Depending on the type of service you are providing, you may want to denote who covers extra costs incurred such as fees for postage and phone calls.

→ **Include delivery format information.** Will you deliver the first draft electronically? However you choose to deliver the material, state it.

→   **Specify about revisions.** This is a huge part of the con-
    tract, because if you do not state how many rounds of
    revisions are included (or what will be charged for extra
    rounds if needed), you can wind up having to revise the
    work as many times as the client demands. Most freelanc-
    ers include one to three rounds of revisions in their work
    and bill at an hourly rate for more than the number of
    revisions agreed to.

→   **Include an exit strategy.** In the event things are not work-
    ing out, most contracts state that either you or the client
    can terminate the agreement, or that you have to both
    agree to go separate ways. Be sure if you include this sec-
    tion to add a clause about monies owed for work com-
    pleted; if you dissolve the agreement before the work is
    done, you should be paid for the work you completed up
    to the point the contract ended.

→   **Specify your status.** In most cases, you will want to denote
    your status, which is likely an "independent contractor,"
    depending what state you live in.

→   **Denote potential contract changes.** If the scope of work
    changes or the client wants additional services, state how
    you will update the contract (or just create another).

→   **Address potential disputes.** If a dispute occurs, will you
    try to resolve the matter via arbitration or mediation? If
    either party files a lawsuit, what state rules govern the
    litigation?

→   **Add legal fee information.** In the event that either party
    would dispute the agreement, it's a good idea to add a
    clause specifying who would pay an attorney's fees. If you
    sued the other party and won, a provision in your contract
    could enable you to secure a lawyer without paying an up-
    front retainer. If you think you could violate the contract
    (say you are bad with deadlines and miss the one stated in

the contract), you may want to skip this clause—but the client may not.

→ **Sign off.** Include areas to sign and date.

Just because you can draft a contract without paying a lawyer doesn't mean you shouldn't take advantage of certain resources. Visit *www.nolo.com* to look at sample agreements and check out legal-related guidebooks.

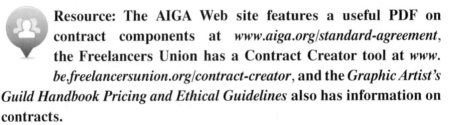 **Resource: The AIGA Web site features a useful PDF on contract components at** *www.aiga.org/standard-agreement*, **the Freelancers Union has a Contract Creator tool at** *www. be.freelancersunion.org/contract-creator*, **and the** *Graphic Artist's Guild Handbook Pricing and Ethical Guidelines* **also has information on contracts.**

Using a Client's Contract

From time to time, a client may suggest you sign their contract instead. Make sure to carefully review the client's contract to make sure it offers the protections you require and does not solely favor the client's interests. For example, if it mentions indemnification, you could be held responsible for any damages if problems occur. For example, let's say that you create a logo and someone sues your client related to the logo. If you indemnify the client, or hold him or her "harmless," you take responsibility for legal costs—totally not what you want. An indemnification clause isn't the end of the world if it is worded to give you enough protection where you feel comfortable, and you can certainly sign a contract that contains one.

In addition to a standard contract, there are two standard agreements that a client may want you to sign, and it is important to understand how both of them work.

→ **Non-compete agreement.** This agreement states you won't work for competitors, which can be tricky if you work in a niche industry. If the client insists on it, you may want to request the agreement specifies you will not perform the same services for competitors while you are working on the client's project. For additional protection, you can specify these competitors by name in your agreement. It's understandable that a client doesn't want you sharing sensitive information with the competition, but you have to make sure if you sign one of these that you aren't limiting your potential at the same time.

→ **Non-disclosure agreement.** Also known as an NDA or confidentiality agreement, a client may require this before sharing confidential information. These agreements are fairly standard; just read it fully before you sign. Then, make sure to stay tight-lipped.

One Contract, Multiple Projects

I commonly run into this issue with my contract: The client signs the contract for one project (say, Web site content writing) then wants to retain me for another (such as writing a brochure).

Taking the time to prepare another contract can stall a project, and add more administrative tasks for both sides. If you can, you may be able to note in the agreement that additional project scopes and agreements can be made while still governed by the same contract parameter and are noted in an addendum.

Michelle Goodman (*www.anti9to5guide.com*), a writer from Seattle who has penned *The Anti 9-to-5 Guide* and *My So-Called Freelance Life*, says she typically signs an initial contract and then updates it over e-mail. "A lot of people just do it that way," she says.

Goodman says she uses e-mail to stipulate terms for subsequent projects or drafts an addendum that the client can approve with an e-mail message confirmation.

When you receive multiple projects from one client, it's best to define things broadly. Perhaps you can state a fee or fee range for specific types of deliverables or services, or note that you and the client can forge separate agreements for individual projects, which will be governed by the same basic terms of the contract to cover things like payments and revisions.

Leverage Your Contract to Protect Yourself

When Kansas-based copywriter Julie Cortés (*www.juliecortes.com*) started freelancing about 15 years ago, she didn't understand the basic rights freelancers have. Now that she's been around the block, she says having a contract is helpful if she needs to dispute a client's actions or inactions.

"Advertising is a very subjective business. A client could either love or hate your work. That's their opinion, and they're entitled to that," Cortés explains. "But that shouldn't affect the outcome of your business agreement. If they hire you to do the work, and you do the work to the best of your ability there's no reason they shouldn't pay you—whether they end up using your work or not. They are paying for a service, not a product."

That's just one of the industry standards that make it into her contract. "Those who want to balk when it's time to pay have no recourse; they signed a legally binding document," she notes. "They may try, but then they'd hear from my attorney...and I'd get paid. I may not ever hear from that client again, but really, who wants to do work with someone as unethical as that anyway?"

Unfortunately, Cortés hears from too many freelancers who have gotten stiffed by clients because they didn't realize they could protect themselves with a simple one- or two-page document. Once you possess this knowledge, and communicate and enforce your rights, you can undoubtedly prevent some headaches and weed out risky clients at the same time.

No Signature? No Problem!

We've talked a lot about contracts thus far—you definitely must have one, and that's one of the few things about freelancing that is very black and white.

But what happens when you are not comfortable with the terms the client wants? Well, friends, that's where the beauty of freelancing comes in because you can turn down a gig.

Claudine Hellmuth (*www.collageartist.com*), an illustrator and artist from Washington, D.C., recalls a time when she refused to sign a contract for a magazine. In her case, it wasn't because she thought she was above using a contract; instead, the terms of the deal just were not worth it.

"They wanted all rights to the artwork which was just silly; they only needed rights to produce it in their magazine and online," she says. The magazine refused to change the contract, and Hellmuth tried to encourage the publication to negotiate terms of the contract. Unfortunately, the magazine would not budge and Hellmuth had to let the deal go. She was sad, but refused to compromise.

I know plenty of freelancers who, despite an alluring sum of money, will stick to their guns when it comes to rights. It looks like Hellmuth made the right decision. That's the kind of power that comes with understanding legal matters—in most cases, it's not as confusing as you may think and the peace of mind you can attain by staying in control is priceless.

Who should have the rights to the work I produce?

"In a perfect world you would have the rights to your work for each project. However, there are times this will not be the case. The first instance is when you are an employee and you create the work for your employer and are acting within your job description. The second is when the work is considered a 'work for hire' under the U.S. Copyright Act. Finally, the client may insist that they get the rights to your work, and for business reasons you decide to take the job."

—Kiffanie Stahle, lawyer, *www.stahlelaw.com*

Protecting Your Rights—and Your Work— With Copyright

According to the U.S. Copyright Office, copyright is defined under Title 17 of the *U.S. Code* as "a form of protection provided by the laws of the United States to the authors of original works of authorship, including literary, dramatic, musical, artistic, and certain other intellectual works." Copyright protection applies to both published and unpublished works.

The Internet is a breeding ground for copyright infringement. I have originated content for clients only to have it ripped off by competitors, and I know plenty more creative folks whose work has been copied and shared without their permission. From ripped-off logos to copied-and-pasted content, solo-pros have every right to be concerned about unauthorized use of their work.

Many of us have had our work shared without permission, or perhaps a client wants all the original artwork files to his or her project. Who governs this sort of thing?

The moment I put my words on a page, I have a copyright in the material. To give me added protection, however, I must register my content. The same goes for a graphic artist who creates a logo, for example.

If someone replicates or distributes your work without your consent, you have a few different legal avenues to take that depend on when you register the work.

Let's say someone other than my client reposts Web site content I have written for the client, but I did not register it with the U.S. Copyright Office. In response, I could send a Digital Millennium Copyright Act (DMCA) takedown notice or have a lawyer write a cease and desist letter. I could also decide I want to sue the person who reproduced my work. Kiffanie Stahle (*www.stahlelaw.com*), a California-based lawyer who specializes in copyright and intellectual property, says it can be more difficult to find an attorney and sue if the work is not registered before infringement, though that can depend on the case.

In this hypothetical case, because I did not register the content until after infringement, I could receive the damages I suffered, such as my licensing fee and any profits the infringing party collected.

On the other hand, if I had I registered the content before the infringing party posted it, I could get statutory damages. I wouldn't have to prove what the infringing party profited from my content; I could just get money based on the fact that the person took a registered work.

I could also require that person to cover my attorney fees along with the costs incurred due to the trial. To qualify for statutory damages, I would have had to register my work with the U.S. Copyright Office before the infringement or within three months of it.

This is where that all-important contract comes in, yet again. *You need to spell out who owns the preliminary concepts and designs, as well as the final deliverables. You also want to specify whether or not you can use the final materials in your portfolio or in industry competitions.*

Resource
Check out *www.plagiarismtoday.com*, a blog covering content theft and more.

Help! Someone ripped off my work. What are my legal options?

"Your options vary based on who ripped off your work, what they did with it, how you feel about it, and if your work is registered with the U.S. Copyright Office. Depending on each of the above factors, you may consider: (1) doing nothing, (2) sending a DMCA take-down notice, (3) sending a cease and desist letter, either from you or from an attorney, (4) filing a lawsuit for copyright infringement."

—Kiffanie Stahle, lawyer, *www.stahlelaw.com*

Making the Case for Copyright Infringement

A lot of solo-pros that I spoke with while putting together this book insist that copyright law doesn't do enough to protect them.

Oregon-based illustrative designer Von Glitschka (*www.vonglitschka.com*) has found many instances of artwork he created for clients being sold by others making money off his creativity. In most cases, Glitschka's clients don't even know they have been ripped off, but Glitschka keeps tabs on these "weasels," as he calls them.

He believes the problem with copyright law is that unless you legally copyright each piece of artwork, you don't have much of a platform to protect yourself. Glitschka doesn't copyright most of his designs. To do so, he says, would be time-consuming and could get expensive because he originates so many visuals. "Who can realistically do that other than large multi-national corporations?"

Even though he does not copyright the majority of his work, it continues to show up on logo mill Web sites and is being sold to companies across the globe—so Glitschka devotes some of his time to weasel-tracking in order to try to protect himself and his clients.

Resource
The Digital Millennium Copyright Act (DMCA), started in 1998, offers guidelines on copyright law for digital material. Learn more about it at *www.copyright.gov*.

Must-Read
Steal Like an Artist: 10 Things Nobody Told You About Being Creative **by Austin Kleon**

Legal Recourse for Copyright Infringement

What happens when you need to take action against someone for copyright infringement?

If you find your copyright has been infringed upon via a Web site, you want to contact the owner of the infringing site, the host of the infringing site, and search engines that are linking to the infringing site.

If the *owner* of a Web site infringes on your material, they should receive a *cease and desist letter*. But if the owner has allowed a third party to infringe on your copyright, it is possible they should be sent a *DMCA letter*. DMCA letters can be used for both the owner and another Web site. It's sent to the Web host of a site, not the actual owner. If your client uses your material incorrectly, a lawyer could also send a cease and desist letter, but the cease and desist letter could also be sent to another party.

You can search on-line for templates to see what these notifications look like. Even if you do not hire a lawyer when you start your business, it's a good idea to have some local resources in mind. If you ever need to issue one of these notifications, the lawyer can help draft the letter or give you other resources so you can respond in a timely fashion.

Resolving Disputes Legally

Legal snafus encompass more than just copyright. Let's say a client breaks your written agreement in any fashion. (Not paying up is a big one—it's happened to me a few times!) Stahle recommends small claims court to resolve such disputes.

You don't need to hire an attorney to go to small claims court; you just gather your evidence and applicable documents, and present it before a judge. "It really is a good low-cost option for artists to recover money from people," Stahle says. If you need to collect money from a company or person and use a small claims court, most states give you up to 10 years to collect payments, she adds.

Another action you may take if a client is playing "hide the paycheck" with you is to hire a collections agency. This is typically a last-ditch effort for many freelancers because the agency will take about half of the money they recover. A lot of creative professionals I know who have used collections agencies do so not caring that the agent will charge them half their outstanding fee—but do so based on the principle that a client skipping out on payment isn't cool.

Before you go all Elle Woods on people, remember that sometimes a simple notification letter will work to alert a client that a payment is late, or inform a Web site that what they are passing off as theirs really belongs to you. I recently had a client who saw that the content I originated for him had been copied and pasted nearly word for word on another site (he used *www.copyscape.com* to verify). Luckily, the client knew my work was original; I spell out in my contract that it will be, plus the date the copied text was posted was long after mine was created. He sent a cease and desist letter to the outfit and the content was taken down immediately.

Remember: The owner of a Web site or other outfit where your work has been copied or shared may not be aware it was stolen; they could have hired another freelancer that swiped your work and said he or she created it. It's always a good idea to start off polite in any correspondence—at least in the first letter!

Thinking in Terms of a "Drive-By"

If you listen to the Freelance Radio podcast, you may be familiar with the official "Kristen Fischer method" of collecting payment. Always one to infuse my "New Jersey–ness" into the banter on the show, I commonly joke about doing a drive-by to the office of a client that has not paid up after countless attempts to collect an outstanding balance. (A *drive-by* refers to a drive-by shooting. In my case, I used to get so angry when I couldn't collect payment that I wanted to get in the car and stalk—not shoot—the client—though some made me wish I owned an AK-47.)

Now, I've never driven by a client's office if they haven't paid up; I don't even own a gun. When I say on the podcast that "sometimes you just have to do a drive-by" it's more so about taking a tough-girl stance, armed with nothing but a firm, yet professional, demeanor.

I'm persistent. Very persistent. Whereas some creative freelancers would give up on collecting payment after sending an invoice and a follow-up notice, I tend to get in the client's face a little, so to speak. I've gone as far as to contact higher-ups in a company about an outstanding invoice, or to e-mail and fax the invoice several times. Persistence can be very useful when you think all hope is lost. I used to get very fired up (no pun intended, but a good one) when payments were late. Most of the time, clients were simply late on payments, but I did get burned a few times and chose not to take more legal action because the balances were on the low side.

If a client has ever stiffed you, you probably can understand why I reference the term "drive-by." Sometimes you're so angry about not getting paid that you want to just shoot someone! Don't do that, though. Actually, don't even drive by the client's office, even though you may want to walk in there and slam your invoice down on the project manager's desk.

Instead, be persistent and, only if needed, take legal action. You have all the tools at your disposal to protect and stand up for yourself as a creative professional. There is absolutely no need to resort to violence, but if you need to go for a jog or play a game of *Halo* to release some aggression, by all means go for it. I like to take things into my own hands for as long as I can without going the legal route. My persistence can turn into annoyance most of the time, and I usually collect the money I'm owed.

If you have sent numerous inquiries about overdue payment, for example, the client may respond after a few attempts, and you may be able to work things out amicably or set up a payment plan. With a little persistence, you may be able to collect payment on an invoice that would have otherwise gone unpaid. In reality, you don't "drive by" at all. (I just like to think I'm a tough gal.)

In fact, once you build your business and establish boundaries, you will hopefully find that you don't deal with too many issues pertaining to outstanding balances. Copyright? That may become more of an issue as your talent develops because, well, even weasels have a good eye for art.

The Lowdown on Legal Issues

If you run into a legal matter through the course of doing business, try not to panic. Whether someone rips off your work and you send them a DMCA notice, or your need to retain a lawyer because a client hasn't paid their bill, it's not the end of the world.

Remember that legal issues are overwhelming for just about everyone—even some lawyers! I leave it up to you to determine what action you take—if you ever have to. The majority of freelancers will be just fine simply having a contract in place. Should something arise, however, now you're prepared to take action.

Here's my biggest takeaway for this chapter: Have a contract. If you do nothing else, make sure you take time to draft a simple contract and use it every time you work with a client. It's the foundation for the protection you deserve as an artistic professional.

Sweet Success
Imitation Is Not the Sincerest Form of Flattery
Von Glitschka (*www.vonglitschka.com*), an illustrative designer from Oregon, has found his designs copied on numerous Web sites. Seeking legal recourse, he has had to hire a copyright lawyer in the past.

Glitschka shares some of his tales at *www.drawsigner.com*. When he notices work is stolen, he contacts the infringing party with a DMCA letter, which requests the work be removed right away. It's also a good idea to send the letter to the infringing Web site's hosting service as well, he says. Most of the time, the work is removed promptly.

Glitschka doesn't copyright every design or logo he creates, but he says it is useful to put a few images on a single standard sheet of paper and have the group of images copyrighted for the same fee that the U.S. Copyright Office would charge per image.

"I've tried to cherry-pick the artwork I think is most vulnerable to infringement and once every quarter send off a sheet to get them protected," he says.

Beginner Mishap
Get it in Writing

When she first started freelancing, Seattle-based writer Michelle Goodman (*www.anti9to5guide.com*) had a client who referred her to a well-known author who had penned books on dating, relationships, and sex. Goodman was excited to work for such a notable writer, adapting information from the books into content for an audio format.

The problem? She didn't have a contract in place. "I think we agreed to something very loosey-goosey over e-mail," Goodman recalls, adding that she did not require a deposit before starting the project.

The author kept changing her mind on what Goodman was producing about halfway through each project. Sometimes, the author didn't even see the work Goodman produced before ix-naying it. "This happened multiple times, and anyone who works in creative stuff knows clients do this," she adds.

As a rookie, Goodman did what many novices do: anything to please the client. Without a contract in place, she did not feel comfortable speaking up to the author about excessive revisions and project reboots.

The project kind of died out after a while, and Goodman doesn't recall if she was completely reimbursed for her services. She says the experience, however, taught her how to stand up for herself—and to have a written agreement in place that backs her up.

Chapter 4

Finances for Freelancers

When I set out to write this book, I knew it would have to include a chapter on financial matters. After all, once you are earning money, you have to properly document and retain what comes in—and what goes out.

Luckily for creative professionals, we have accountants, tax preparers, enrolled agents, and tax software to help us make sense of the numbers. You can certainly hire a financial professional to offer advice and even tabulate your taxes, but you still have to know the financial basics of how a business runs.

Keep in mind as you read this chapter that I have broken everything down so it is easy to read, understand, and apply. That said, it's a general overview. I cannot provide too many specifics, but I can give you the foundation you need so you can take charge of your finances, and spend less time with the calculator and more time with the canvas.

It is sort of a given that a creative professional doesn't want to spend time tracking checks that come in or saving receipts for tax deductions. I'll admit: I sort of detest doing those things. Yet if you know how to properly organize your financial records, it will make everything much easier come tax time. In fact, your business will function smoothly all year long because you will know where you stand, be able to stay on top of obligations, make informed choices, and do your all to stay protected legally.

Must-Read
The Creative Professional's Guide to Money: How to Think About It, How to Talk About it, How to Manage It **by Ilise Benun**

Hiring Out vs. Using Tax Software

I mentioned hiring an accountant or tax preparer, and that is music to the ears of many freelancers. It is wonderful to be able to hand off the tasks you don't enjoy doing. Trust me: You're not any less of a businessperson if you do not handle your accounting or bookkeeping. But that doesn't mean you can afford not to understand the basic gist of how it all works because, at the end of the day, *you* are responsible for your finances.

I knew very little about tracking expenses when I began my business. I knew how to create a log to track invoices and payments. I saved business-related receipts for things such as postage and paper. That was about all I knew how to do. I hired an accountant to help me not only file my taxes, but to get a grip on how to manage the financial and recordkeeping aspects of my business. At the time, I dreaded dealing with money and only cared that I paid my rent each month.

That was a big year with lots of changes. I had started my own business, became engaged, and gotten married. Then, a year later, Tim and I purchased our first house. If owning my business wasn't enough, money would now play a more prominent role in my life. I was forced to learn what terms such as *deductible* and *escrow* meant. (One can only evade it for so long!)

I used the accountant for the first two years of my business. The information she gave me was invaluable; in fact, she was helpful in educating Tim about the accounting process, something he was always intrigued by. (I contend that's because he has only ever worked one job at a time!)

The accountant expanded my knowledge of what expenses were deductible, and showed me how to organize files and prepare my taxes. I didn't know everything about accounting—and still do not—but I knew what files to retain and what expenses to deduct. Tim has taken over our taxes ever since and oddly enough enjoys it.

Most freelancers still use accountants every year, which is quite valuable because taxes are complicated, and new rules come up every year. But you do not have to rely on an accountant to handle your bookkeeping and/or accounting. I recommend doing so for the first few years, especially to master taxes, but after that, you can decide if you want to keep handing off your accounting and bookkeeping or if you want to tackle it yourself (or pawn it off on an unsuspecting spouse!).

Keep in mind as you read that I am tailoring my message to Americans so I will reference the Internal Revenue Service, or IRS, as the government tax agency.

What can I expect if I hire an accountant? Approximately how much will it cost?

"Accountants and tax preparers come in all shapes and sizes. As with any professional service, ask your questions before you engage. Some questions I would ask:

1. *Do you charge a fixed rate, hourly, or 'by the form'? Describe your scenario and ask for an estimate.*

2. *Is there any follow-up consultation included? Is there a charge if I call you with a question in a few months? Will you prepare estimated tax vouchers if needed?*

3. *What is the charge if you need to 'clean up my books' first? If your books are a mess the tax preparation will take longer and be more expensive. The professional may simply say, 'Come back when you are organized.'*

4. *Make sure your expectations are realistic. If you just want a no-hassle tax prep for a cheap price, don't expect a CPA at your doorstep explaining every line item. If you want extensive guidance, say that at the outset and be prepared to pay for it."*

—Richard Streitfeld, accountant,
www.peaceloveandbusinessplanning.com

Tracking Payments and Expenses

Accounting is not all about taxes. It includes documenting and tracking expenses, but also managing records such as invoices. Bookkeeping is the act of recording financial transactions, and that can include sales, purchases, income, receipts, and payments. Accounting includes bookkeeping but is more about the reporting of financial information as you will do with your taxes.

One thing is key for both aspects of financial management: You will need to be meticulous when it comes to documenting both income and expenses. For example, once I knew that I could deduct fuel for work-related travel, I hung on to those receipts like glue.

I know plenty of creative professionals that are big into technology. If you have listened to my Freelance Radio podcasts, you know that co-hosts Von and Dickie are big into the newest gadgets, whereas I am more old-school. I've learned that a good blend of paper documents and digital records is a smart mix to track your payments and expenses. That is, you may want to invest in a file folder to hang on to receipts and handle all of your payments using software such as QuickBooks. Point is, you have to keep track of money coming in and going out of your business—however you want to work it.

Another tip related to this is to have a separate bank account for your business. It makes sense because this route makes you appear more professional, especially if you are writing checks. A separate checking account also makes it easy to demonstrate your financial transparency in the event of a tax audit and can make tax time easier because you won't have to separate out business expenses from personal outlays. In separating bank accounts, you can also more easily monitor the financial results for your business.

 Resource
Check out *www.shoeboxed.com*, a tool that lets you scan and track receipts—and integrate the feature with the accounting software FreshBooks.

The Financial Income and Tax Model for Freelancers

The first thing to understand about how to manage your income and taxes is that you will report them differently than you did when you may have worked a traditional job. At your old job, you would receive one W-2 form at the end of the year and plug in those figures to complete your taxes.

As a self-employed professional, however, you most likely will collect from multiple clients. Most clients will give you a 1099 form at the end of the year for all the projects you have worked on, but some don't have to, depending on what type of business they are. In fact, a client is not required to send a 1099 form if the work was less than $600, if you are incorporated, or if you are an LLC. To sum up, instead of one W-2, you will probably have several 1099s. It gets confusing because you still have to report for clients that do not send 1099s. In fact, you need to report *all* income you make to the IRS—hence the need to *track everything*.

At the end of the year, you will have to match up payments you earned from clients that sent you 1099s with the amount on the forms. Then, as I said, you have to report on the income from clients that did not send you 1099s. This is why it's good to have a system that tracks all of your income, regardless of whether it is from a client that sends 1099s or not.

Unfortunately, the money you get from clients is not yours alone. Why? Because you must pay taxes on it! So you're going to owe the federal and state government some money—that's *income tax*.

In addition to the income tax, there is a second tax you'll also be assessed just for going solo: the *self-employment tax*, which is equivalent to the Social Security and Medicare taxes that were withheld from the paycheck you earned if you were employed traditionally. There, you split the cost of Social Security and Medicare taxes with your employer. When you are a freelancer, however, you have to pay both portions. The good thing is that you pay taxes on your income after, or net of, expenses, which employees with W-2 status cannot.

Must-Read
Working for Yourself: Law & Taxes for Independent Contractors, Freelancers & Consultants by **Stephen Fishman**

Ponying Up to Uncle Sam

By now you probably know that you're going to wind up owing the government money because you are not having taxes withheld on the income you collect. You have two choices: pay up at the end of the tax year (a huge lump sum) or pay quarterly (four smaller payments). You'll be paying the same amount of money you owe—you can't change that. If you pay quarterly, however, you tend to avoid financial penalties. Plus, you won't owe an overwhelming amount of money at the end of the year.

The type of tax return you file depends on the business structure you choose. We went over the types of business structures you can choose from in Chapter 2. Now we'll review some basics about taxes.

Quarterly Taxes

Perhaps I should contribute my own "beginner mishap" story like you have read in other chapters. During my first year, I did not know what to expect with my taxes. By the time I hired an accountant, I had already worked a full year and was making a pretty impressive income. I didn't know that I should pay quarterly taxes; I thought I could only pay a huge chunk at the end of the year. As a result, I got stuck paying several thousand dollars in taxes. It was like my own personal financial apocalypse, because that was just about the same time as Tim and I were closing on our house and also owed the down payment, an even bigger sum of money.

Lesson learned: I began paying quarterly taxes.

Quarterly payments are based on estimates of what you owe—your self-employment tax and your income tax. Because an employer will not withhold these taxes for you, you can use Form 1040-ES: Estimated Tax for Individuals to see if you have to file quarterly taxes. The form includes vouchers you submit (just as you would with, say, your electricity bill) with the payment. You can also make some payments using the Electronic Federal Tax Payment System (EFTPS).

Let's say this is your first year as a solopreneur. You will need to estimate the amount of income you plan on earning. If you estimate too high or low, you just complete another Form 1040-ES worksheet to refigure your estimated tax for the next quarter. In the event you underestimate what you will owe and wind up overpaying, the IRS will return the money or you can credit it to your estimated taxes for the next year. In short, if you know you will owe more than $1,000, it is generally advisable to pay quarterly estimated taxes.

If you have tax records from previous years of self-employment, you can base your estimations on the previous year. (When my accountant did my taxes, she did all the estimations for me and gave me the vouchers pre-completed. Most tax software programs can also pre-estimate what you will owe in taxes so you can prepare your vouchers ahead of time.)

The general rule of thumb is that you can incur penalties if you have not paid your quarterly taxes (also known as estimated taxes) at the same rate that you did the year before. To avoid penalties and make nice with the IRS, pay your taxes quarterly, pay the right amount, and make those payments on time.

What happens if I don't pay quarterly, but am supposed to?

"You will not go to jail for not paying in a timely fashion, but you will be penalized for not paying throughout the year as a W-2 employee would. You are expected to pay 'ratably' throughout the year. (There is an exception for seasonal income and major fluctuations, but that requires additional filings and may not be worth the effort.)

The penalties are one consequence (and they apply to state underpayments as well). The calendar for making estimated tax payments is not a calendar year. In fact, the first payment is due April 15. So if Paul the Piper owes $5,000 on April 15, 2013 for the 2012 tax year—and doesn't have it—then guess what? He also won't have the money for the first payment on his 2013 income, due the same date. It is really hard to dig yourself out of such a hole!

The IRS does not care what pocket you pay the taxes out of. So if you do have a W-2 job in addition to your freelance income, you can increase your withholdings from that job, or from a spouse's W-2 (assuming you are going to file jointly), to cover the liability."

—Richard Streitfeld, accountant,
www.peaceloveandbusinessplanning.com

Filing Your Annual Tax Return

Even if you do make quarterly payments like a star freelancer, you still have to file an annual return. To file your annual income tax return, you will need to use Schedule SE (Form 1040). You also have to file either a Schedule C or Schedule C-EZ. According to the IRS, small businesses and statutory employees with less than $5,000 in expenses may be able to file Schedule C-EZ instead of Schedule C. To find out if you can use Schedule C-EZ, check the form.

In order to report your self-employment tax, you have to file Schedule SE (Form 1040), which covers the self-employment tax. Use the figures you report on Schedule C or Schedule C-EZ to calculate the amount in self-employment taxes that are due on that income.

What was your biggest financial mishap as a freelancer starting out?

"My big rookie mistake when I began my freelance writing business was underestimating my tax obligation. When you're working for a company, income tax is pretty much invisible to you: It's deducted automatically from your paycheck, and you only think about it in April. I knew I would be on the hook for 15 percent self-employment tax as an indie writer, but I underestimated the percentage of income tax I'd also owe quarterly. The first meeting with my accountant was an eye-opener, and it revealed to me how very important it is to deduct (legitimately) as many business expenses as possible to reduce taxable income."

—Bryn Mooth, freelance writer, *www.brynmooth.com*

Resource
Find IRS tax forms at *www.irs.gov/formspubs/index.html*.

All About the "A Word" (Audits)

According to the IRS, if you report a negative figure on your Schedule C form for more than two out of five years, you can be subject to the Hobby Loss Rule of Thumb. This pretty much means that the IRS can decide your business is actually just a hobby, which can set you up for an audit. There are a variety of factors that can make you an easy target for the dreaded IRS audit.

"Just because you had continuous losses does not mean the IRS would disqualify you," notes Richard Streitfeld (*www.peaceloveand-businessplanning.com*), an accountant based in Rhode Island.

Audit is the buzz kill word in the freelance world. It doesn't mean you are in trouble, but the IRS can examine your files with a fine tooth comb and come down pretty hard if they find any discrepancies.

Now, because you are self-employed as a creative professional, you may not have any major losses if you keep your overhead low and earn enough money. Unlike a small business with a storefront, products, and employees, you probably do not have to spend thousands to get your business running and you can probably work from home. Perhaps you need a new computer, or software. Maybe you need art supplies. It's quite different than the outlay would be if you were forming a small business that required a physical setting, such as a restaurant or shop. Still, it is good to have an eye on keeping your overhead low and avoiding financial losses.

Another audit trigger is if you are not properly claiming deductions. We'll delve into what's legitimate to deduct, or subtract, off your income in just a bit so you can avoid that.

Keep in mind that "correspondence audits" are another type of audit where you simply send in documentation. The IRS can also randomly audit you, so if you get a notice, it doesn't necessarily mean you have done something wrong. Audits are, unfortunately, a part of life for many people—not just creatives. Ensuring you are properly deducting expenses and reporting income is the best audit-preparedness method possible.

What's Deductible?

All the financial talk can be deafening. I have found the only positive with taxes, because I never get money back from the government, is to focus on deductions. It makes me happy to legitimately deduct money that Uncle Sam can't tax me on. Without deductions, I'd pay a heck of a whole lot more in taxes. This is why I love deductions almost as much as my nieces and my nephew!

Tax deductions are amounts of money that you can subtract from your overall income. The more you deduct, within reason, the less money you pay taxes on.

If you are in business to make a profit, the IRS says you can deduct business expenses that are *ordinary* and *necessary*. The IRS defines an *ordinary expense* as a common or accepted expense in your trade or business. A *necessary expense* is one that is helpful and appropriate for your trade. The IRS states that an expense does not have to be indispensable to be considered necessary.

Deductions must relate to your business (most creative professionals use computers, a completely legitimate deduction). In the event that your cell phone is for business and personal use, you have to keep records (or a log) to show that. Same thing if you use your personal vehicle to visit client offices—gotta have those records.

Expenses you can deduct are kind of self-explanatory. For example, you purchase ink for your printer (assuming you use the printer for work), or you purchase a new phone for your home office—deductible. You renew your membership to a trade organization in your industry— another deduction. Some are more complicated, such as your utilities. My home office accounts for about 20 percent of my home, so I can't deduct all of the gas, electricity, and water we use in our home, but I can deduct 20 percent from each bill through the home office deduction. If you are producing a tangible product for sale—say, a painting on a canvas—you can deduct the cost for art supplies. Just keep the receipts.

You have to be careful with deductions; it's tempting to want to deduct just about everything. Whatever you deduct, though, you have to *back up with receipts*. And even if you have a receipt for something you deduct, it can still signal a red flag to the IRS. You want to make sure that whatever you deduct, it doesn't sound fishy. After all, I work best with music on, but I cannot justify iTunes expenses as a must-have to the IRS. Well, I can try, but I'm going to go ahead and say that it probably wouldn't go so well. Make sure you can justify "iffy" deductions!

Common Deductions for Self-Employed Professionals

The following is a basic list of typical expenses freelancers deduct:

→ Office or art supplies

→ Transportation (cab and bus fare, etc.)

→ Book, magazines and reference material

→ Telephone/Internet

→ Business insurance

→ Promotion (brochures, business cards, etc.)

→ Office rent.

→ Gas, electricity, water, mortgage/rent

→ Professional memberships

→ Postage

→ Tax preparation (software or accountant fees)

→ Travel

→ Business meals and entertainment

→ Equipment (including repairs/maintenance)

→ Health insurance

→ Web site costs (domain registration, hosting, etc.)

→ Software

→ Legal and professional fees

Until you know for sure what is deductible, I recommend consulting a tax professional. Compile a list of questions about what deductions you can claim and bring the list to your accountant.

There are a few gray areas when it comes to what's deductible. For example, travel expenses are deductible if you meet a client or attend a conference, but the event must be primarily for business and you must be away for at least one night.

Let's say you attend a business event such as the Creative Freelancer Conference. You spend two days at the conference and stay an extra day to do some sightseeing. You can deduct all of your expenses for the duration of the conference (but only 50 percent of meals), but you cannot deduct expenses for the extra night you stayed, the enormous brunch you scarfed down the day after the conference, or the museum you visited to work off the calories. The rules get more complicated if you travel more than seven days or take your family with you, so be sure to consult a tax professional for advice.

When it comes to deductions, you almost always have to learn as you go. After a few years, you'll be certain which receipts to save, what you can deduct, and (unfortunately in the case of my iTunes obsession) what you cannot. I would hang on to any receipt that you think could be a business-related deduction until you *know* what is allowed.

Claudine Hellmuth (*www.collageartist.com*), an illustrator and artist from Washington, D.C., says she never deducts things that could raise a red flag for an audit; it's not worth the stress. "I am very careful with my deductions because I am crazy paranoid about getting audited," she confesses.

"I learned I can't deduct new clothes for when I go on TV which I think is a real bummer because usually I wouldn't be buying these clothes if I wasn't going on TV," she notes.

What expenses are not deductible for a creative freelancer?

"The phrase 'reasonable and necessary' to run your business gives you wide latitude. That does not usually mean you can deduct what is reasonable and necessary for you to go to work and function as a professional. Commuting to your office: Nope. Food at work: Your daily brown bag lunch or take out from fast food joints—usually not. Exception: You go out with a colleague or prospect, or you are overnight on a business trip. Your daily cup o' Joe from Starbucks: No! Unless you are there discussing business with someone."

—Richard Streitfeld, accountant,
www.peaceloveandbusinessplanning.com

Depreciation

The idea behind depreciation is that certain purchases generate income over a number of years. Hence, you cannot deduct the purchase of, let's say, a $1,000,000 rental property in one year. But there are instances where you can deduct all your asset purchases; some common ones for freelancers are computers and cameras.

According to Stephen Fishman's book *Working for Yourself: Law & Taxes for Independent Contractors, Freelancers & Consultants*, you must spread depreciation over more than one year on the purchase of an asset if:

→   You use the item (or property) less than 51 percent of the time for your business.

→   The item is a property that you converted for business use.

→   The property has a structure located on it.

→   A relative sold the item to you.

→   You used a trade-in to finance the purchase.

→   You inherited the item or it was a gift.

→ The item is an intangible asset (a trademark, patent, or copyright).

→ It is a heating or air conditioning unit.

Another benefit to using depreciation is if you want to show maximum taxable income for the year by spreading the expense out over several years. This is particularly useful if your business has incurred a loss or not been profitable, and could be considered a hobby. It is also a good strategy if you want to save some deductions for future years when you may have more income and fewer expenses.

Unless you are able to depreciate the item in one year, you have to depreciate based on how long the item is expected yield value, according to the IRS. The IRS refers to this as an item's "useful life," and it offers a specific table depending on the type of asset. Creative professionals may not do a whole lot of depreciation, but if you own a trademark, it's worth asking your accountant about amortization, which is the equivalent concept for "intangible assets" like trademarks.

Otherwise, you will deduct most expenses every year, and you may never wind up using depreciation, but it's good to know it exists!

Resource
IRS Publication 946: How to Depreciate Property

Plus 1: Hiring Help

Here is another scenario that most creative freelancers may never face, but I think it is important to note. If you choose to hire an independent contractor to farm out some work, keep in mind a few things.

First, make sure you can do that according to any legal agreement you have in place.

As for the tax implications, the IRS is concerned that independent contractors do not report all of their income—or pay taxes on it. So if you hire an unincorporated independent contractor and pay that person $600 or more a year for a business-related service, you must file IRS Form 1099-MISC and denote how much you paid the contractor and display the independent contractor's identification number or Social Security number.

Also, have the contracted worker fill out a W-9 when you hire him or her so you don't have to chase the worker down at the end of the year for that information. If you hire an incorporated independent contractor, you generally do not have to file a 1099 (an exception for lawyers exists), but be prepared because the IRS is asking more questions on tax forms on whether you have used 1099-eligible contractors, Streitfeld advises.

Invoicing and Recordkeeping

In the age of digital everything, it is still important to keep paper *and* electronic records. Establishing how you set up your recordkeeping processes is dependent on what types of methods you embrace, and there is no right way. In my opinion, the best way is to create a process that you can work with. That is, if you work best with a certain software, use it. Just keep in mind that paper will come into play somehow so long as you purchase items that come with paper receipts.

I keep two file cabinets in my office: one for work, and one for my personal documents. It includes files for clients as well as a file for my taxes. Then there is a huge yellow folder for receipts—and it is brimming with them. Because I can deduct a portion of my utilities, I keep separate files for those as well. Some clients pay me in checks, so I retain all of the stubs as well.

Invoicing, however, is done on the computer. I'm pretty high-tech in that respect. At the time I was writing this book, I finally agreed to give in and purchase QuickBooks. I'm going to be in the process of periodically entering receipts into the computer soon, which is a little overwhelming, but I am confident it will make things easier in the long run. I'll still need to hang on to paper receipts and other documentation, but the thought of plugging in a number and having it generate an invoice automatically sounds almost better to me than sipping Starbucks chai tea on a chilly autumn afternoon.

The point in sharing all of this is to let you know that you have to come up with your own system. Whatever that is, just make sure you retain all pertinent records however you want to store them. Nowadays, you can buy gadgets that scan and electronically store receipts so you can have a relatively paperless office.

Good recordkeeping helps me calculate deductions, prepare tax returns, maintain audit preparedness, and accurately monitor the progress of my business. Once you find a system that works for you, it will take the hassle out of bookkeeping and you probably won't dread it as much as before you began your business.

Must-Read
The Money Book for Freelancers, Part-Timers, and the Self-Employed: The Only Personal Finance System for People with Not-So-Regular Jobs **by Joe D'Agnese and Denise Kiernan**

Rollin' With Keeping a Log

Being able to prove your deductions—and deducting only legitimate expenses—is a must. If you do a fair amount of traveling to meet clients and use your own vehicle, it pays to keep a logbook so you can separate personal expenses from business purchases, because you probably use your car for both.

Keep a log to monitor your business travels. Use either your smartphone or a small memo pad to jot down the trip date and purpose, then record your mileage before and after the trip, and compute the number of miles traveled. Streitfeld recommends hanging on to auto shop receipts and jotting down your vehicle's mileage at the beginning and end of the year so it can support what you report on total miles driven during the year.

Keeping a log is not just for traveling in your vehicle, though. You may also want to keep a log for things like business entertainment and meals if those are frequent. I typically keep a small notepad in the console of my car to record these expenses, but if you keep everything on a phone or tablet, just make sure you keep it on you whenever you head out.

Resource
Check out these apps to help you track mileage on the go: Mileage Tracker, Mileage App, Trip Cubby, TripLog/1040, and Trip Master.

How long do I need to hang on to tax documents?

"In general, the IRS has three years from the date your return was filed to audit your return. They also have the right to go back longer if underreporting of income is suspected. If you are self-employed it is recommended to hold on to your receipts and documentation for seven years. Some records should be kept longer if the deductions take place over many years or later."

—Richard Streitfeld, accountant,
www.peaceloveandbusinessplanning.com

Why Think About Retirement When You're Living the Dream?

In addition to finances, I think it is important for freelancers to have some retirement planning information at the ready. Why should you have to consider this, especially if it requires you to spend more money when you may already be cash-strapped? Because you would probably set up an account if you held a traditional job. You need to plan for retirement regardless of who employs you!

When you were employed previously, you probably didn't pay much attention to your retirement planning account or health insurance policy. You probably filled out a few forms to set them up when you started the job and didn't give them much more thought. As a freelancer, however, you will need to arrange these benefits on your own.

I miss donating to my 401(k) and having my employer match the amount I put in. Ah, those were the days. I had some money when I left the company, but I didn't do much with it when I began freelancing. I simply let it sit in the account. I swear, if the money could have spoken up, it would have said how much it missed matching contributions, too!

After a while freelancing, I took that money and rolled it into a Roth IRA. I had to get over the fact that I was in charge of my retirement savings. Now I was not only the account owner but the entity responsible for making contributions; no one would match what I put in anymore.

Even if you have never set up a retirement account or you can't put in a ton of money right now, that's okay. It is sometimes just a good idea to open an account and put a little money in, then add more when you get on your feet.

Resource

Check out the Freelancers Union (*www.freelancersunion.org*), which recently launched its own 401(k) plan. It costs $40 to sign up, and there is an $11 monthly fee, plus a 3 percent administration fee. If you receive 1099 income, you are eligible but you cannot contribute to this plan if you add money to a SEP IRA during the same year.

Individual retirement accounts

Let's talk about the six basic individual retirement account (IRA) options for freelancers: Solo 401(k)s, Traditional IRAs, SIMPLE IRAs, Self-Directed IRAs, SEP IRAs, and Roth IRAs. You'll need to talk to a specialist in the field to find out specifics on each, but this will expose you to some options.

1. **Solo 401(k).** This retirement option is similar to 401(k) plans that you may have had when you were employed, but it is for small business owners. It is limited to the business owner and a spouse and is also known as the Individual 401(k).

    With this option, you can put more money away than a SIMPLE or SEP IRA, and more flexible contribution options exist. In 2012, if you were under the age of 50, you could make a maximum employee deferral contribution of $17,000, plus your business could put in up to a 25-percent profit-sharing donation, up to $50,000. If you were over 50, you could make a maximum employee deferral contribution in the amount of $22,500.

2. **Traditional IRA.** If you earned income and are under the age of 70½, you are eligible to contribute to a Traditional IRA, which is a Personal IRA. In 2012, you could contribute up to $5,000, and $6,000 if you are over 50. Contributions are tax-deductible, which is good news for those of you looking to deduct. Streitfeld notes that freelancers are not eligible if they are covered by a plan at a job that gives you a W-2 at the end of the year. If you are married and your spouse has a W-2 retirement plan, you may not be able to contribute to a Traditional IRA.

    Once you reach age 59½, you can begin taking money out. You are required to withdraw a specified amount yearly beginning the year you turn 70½. If you withdraw from this account early, you're going to likely take a 10-percent penalty and will be taxed on it.

3. **SIMPLE IRA.** A Savings Incentive Match Plan for Employees, or SIMPLE IRA, is pretty straightforward, indeed. Small businesses with fewer than 100 employees that earned $5,000 or more during the previous calendar year are eligible.

    According to *www.BankRate.com*, the cost and complexity for a SIMPLE IRA is low. An employer must match elective deferrals dollar-for-dollar up to 3 percent of a participant's compensation or make a 2-pecent contribution to all employees who earned more than $5,000 during the year. You can open a SIMPLE IRA if you are self-employed; it also can be useful if you wind up expanding and hiring staff members in the future.

4. **Self-Directed IRA.** If you want to put your retirement savings into investments such as real estate or business, you could choose a Self-Directed IRA. It has the same rules as a Traditional IRA, but a few restrictions exist. For instance, if you use the money for personal benefit and are

under 59½, you could put the tax-deferred status of the account at risk. Streitfeld says this option is geared more for savvy investors with a significant amount to spend.

5. **SEP IRA.** A Simplified Employee Pension Individual Retirement Account, or SEP IRA, lets self-employed professionals contribute up to 20 percent of their net self-employment income—up to $50,000 maximum in 2012—into it. If you have employees, check about eligibility and coverage requirements.

6. **Roth IRA.** The maximum contribution you can make to a Roth IRA for 2012 is the same as for a Traditional IRA. Like the Traditional IRA, it is a Personal IRA, too. The contribution allowed remains unchanged from 2011 at $5,000 (or $6,000 if you're 50 or older). Contributions are not deductible; however, your investment grows tax-free and you are not taxed on it when you withdraw it. There are also income limitations depending on your filing status.

   You can split the contribution between your Roth and Traditional IRAs if you choose; any amount equaling $5,000. So if you want to put $2,500 in one account and $2,500 in the other, you can absolutely do so.

There are so many retirement plans out there, so it's best to talk to someone at your bank, an accountant, or a financial planner about your options. If you want to do some research on the plans, I recommend visiting a Web site such as *www.BankRate.com, www.SmartMoney.com,* or *www.irs.gov.*

What's a good retirement option for a creative freelancer starting out who isn't sure if the business will make it?

"If your cash flow can support it there is no harm—and there is clear benefit—in setting up a retirement account in your first year of business. Personal IRAs—Traditional or Roth—are set up outside your

business so there is no effect if the business closes. There are restrictions on eligibility. If you do a SIMPLE IRA or a SEP IRA, these provide tax deductions and can be rolled over into a Personal IRA should your business close or if you are unable to continue the contributions.

If you are thinking you may need that money back soon, then absolutely do not put it in a retirement account; you will get socked with income tax and, most likely, a 10 percent penalty if you need to withdraw it."

—Richard Streitfeld, accountant,
www.peaceloveandbusinessplanning.com

Health Insurance

Like Claudine Hellmuth (*www.collageartist.com*), an illustrator and artist living in Washington, D.C., I am lucky enough to have health insurance through my husband's job. Like her, I wasn't always so fortunate.

Obtaining health insurance is a hot-button issue for creatives, because many of them can't access the plans they held at their former jobs simply because they are not with a company. Individuals can sometimes purchase plans, but the costs are much higher for what would otherwise be more affordable had you stayed in cubicle-ville.

Hellmuth had to pay out-of-pocket for healthcare for a short time when she and her husband were not on the plan through his job. She said it cost about $400 a month for both of them.

I had to do the same after Tim was laid off for a while. I purchased a low-cost plan via *www.ehealthinsurance.com*, but it was basic—like *Dr. Quinn, Medicine Woman* basic. Even she probably offered more care for less.

So how can you acquire a decent health insurance policy? Hellmuth recommends choosing a high-deductible insurance plan to provide basic coverage, especially if you know you'll be on the plan temporarily. I found when I was searching for an independent health plan that the kind of coverage comparable to what I had when I was working in Corporate America ran at least $800 a month for a couple—closer to $1,000 for the really good insurance and even more if you have children, depending on where you live.

As for the "extras" such as dental and vision care, Hellmuth advises passing on them when selecting a temporary plan, because the coverage can be poor. I think it depends which plan you choose. If you are on your own plan for a while, you may be able to purchase basic coverage and then join a discount program for prescription, vision, or dental care. Or take your chances and pay out of pocket. Otherwise, more affordable plans usually do not have the extras unless you pay for them.

Are there positives to paying for your own health insurance? Yes, actually. You can deduct the expenses from your self-employment income. Disadvantage: If you go for the bare-bones coverage and a catastrophe strikes, you may wind up paying a lot.

Buying insurance on your own or via a spouse isn't the only option. You may be able to obtain a policy through a trade organization in your industry, or you can find a health insurance agent to see if he or she can get you better deals.

It is uncertain what will happen in the United States as far as healthcare is concerned. As of this writing, the U.S. government approved plans to move forward with a new healthcare reform platform that will let everyone purchase healthcare, supposedly at a more reasonably priced rate. Some say the plan will be better for self-employed professionals; others say we will be worse off. Like many of you, I'm eagerly awaiting to see how it all turns out.

Resource

Visit *www.healthinsurance.org, www.healthcare.gov, www.ehea lthinsurance.com*, and *www.NASE.org* to learn more about health benefits for self-employed individuals.

Sweet Success
Scoring on Health Insurance

Tim Goldman (*www.timgoldman.com*), a designer and illustrator from New York, knows all about the trials that come with finding health insurance coverage—especially when you don't have an employer to supply it. He went without insurance until his mid-30s.

Goldman once obtained insurance through the Graphic Artists Guild, which at the time offered coverage via a separate entity. He had an even better plan when he got insurance through his partner's employer. Though his Guild insurance was affordable, the employer's plan was more reasonably priced and provided better coverage.

When Goldman's partner left the job, however, they were both without any coverage. "It was up to me to find a way back to insurance for freelancers that I could add my partner on to," he says. Goldman turned to the Freelancers Union, which he says made it fairly easy to sign up (though you have to show paystubs and checks to prove you are working, he notes).

Luckily, he was working at an on-site contract job at the time and had no problem showing documentation. Even better, his partner was able to go on the plan, too.

Beginner Mishap
Taxmageddon

When she started out in the early '90s as a solo-pro, writer Michelle Goodman (*www.anti9to5guide.com*) wasn't concerned about how much she could owe in taxes because she wasn't making much to begin with.

At the time, she had just moved into her own apartment, and was not spending excessively but not making ends meet too well, either. Goodman racked up some debt on her credit card. Tax time came and she didn't pay quarterly, so she owed the full amount of taxes she accrued during the year.

"You start freelancing and you don't make a lot of money, [and] you think, 'I can't owe that much in taxes,' then you owe a year of taxes," says Goodman. "That can be really painful!"

Her intention was never to get out of paying taxes; she just didn't realize *how much* she would owe—nor did she save up for it. Goodman owed the government a few thousand dollars in taxes, and they set her up with a payment plan so she could reimburse them for the outstanding balance.

"It's no joke; you have to pay. And they charge interest...they had the highest interest," she says. "The best thing you can do [to save up for the money you will owe]—and I didn't do this—you should put it [a portion of your earnings] in a savings account and pretend it's not yours."

Chapter 5

Will You Be My Client?

You can create the most gorgeous Web site in the world or design killer business cards, but if you don't have leads to target your marketing to, it won't do much good.

Before you can contact people to see if they are interested in your services, you have to find them. *Lead generation* involves creating interest in what you have to offer, and you can do that by *prospecting*. When people are interested in your services or products, they're known as *prospects*. That's why the terms *lead generation* and *prospecting* often go hand in hand.

Sure, you can drum up business simply by having a Web site; eventually, some people will find it and perhaps they will hire you. You stand a much better chance, however, to get clients (specifically when you are starting out and looking to build a base of customers), if you generate and target leads—and then sell yourself to them. In other words, you have to put in some effort to secure clients.

"Prospecting is *not* about trying to sell your services to strangers. It's about introducing yourself to people who have a likelihood of being interested in your services," notes Canada-based copywriter Steve Slaunwhite, coauthor of *The Wealthy Freelancer: 12 Secrets to a Great Income and an Enviable Lifestyle*.

Engaging the right prospects is a lot like playing football. (Hey, you made it four chapters in without a football analogy from a diehard fan. Let the "game" begin!)

Let me refer to the New England Patriots to illustrate an example. When quarterback Tom Brady has the ball in hand, he is looking for another player to move it into the end zone. Sure, he can hand it off to a running back who will plow through the defense and hopefully gain a couple yards, but the ball can get further it he throws it down the field. In that case, he's ideally looking for one of his receivers to catch it—he wants Wes Welker or Rob Gronkowski to make the catch. He knows the exact guys to target and can pretty much toss the ball right into their hands; then the receiver needs to grip it and run for the end zone.

Targeting the right receivers has earned Brady a pretty impressive reputation as a quarterback. In the same way that Brady eyes Welker or Gronkowski down the field, you have to target the right people before you start selling. Otherwise, you can wind up wasting a lot of time and money on promotional initiatives that go nowhere.

The last thing you want to do is send out hundreds of brochures to companies without specifying the recipient. That's like throwing a Hail Mary toward the end zone and praying that receiver Aaron Hernandez has been hanging out there all along, unblocked, waiting for the ball. Just because he's there doesn't mean he will catch it. That's a complete crapshoot other than those rare occasions when—*bink!*—the catch is made, six points are added to the Pats' score, and I go berserk on my couch celebrating.

Receivers (or prospective clients, in this case) aren't just waiting around for you to contact them. The defense (other creatives, in our case) is always vying for the attention of your targets.

The point is to concentrate your efforts as precisely as possible. Find the right guys to target, make a pass (or sales pitch), and the rest is in their hands. If Welker misses, Brady always has other options to score—just as you always have more chances to nab clients. In short, you have plenty of opportunities to reach viable prospective clients. You just have to figure out which jersey number to target, so to say. In focusing your efforts, you stand a better chance to turn prospects into clients than you would going aimlessly.

Let's talk about some ways to get you into the game—even if football isn't your sport and the Patriots aren't your team.

Must-Read

Clients, Clients, and More Clients: Create and Endless Stream of New Business with the Power of Psychology by **Larina Kase, PsyD**

Who Are Your Clients?

Good marketers realize that half of the effort in marketing is figuring out who the prospects are. You have to approach people who *want* to hear what you have to say.

Take time to think about the clients you want to reach. When I started out, I was eager to focus on marketing and blasted out e-mails to local companies. After a while, I realized I could be more efficient if I thought about the type of projects I wanted and who the people were that could hire me. In selecting companies to pitch, I take time to see who to contact in the marketing department because the human resources department is likely focused more on filling open full-time spots. Sometimes I check out LinkedIn to identify the name of the potential client. Most importantly, I don't just blindly mail a brochure to the corporate headquarters or send a message to the general e-mail address; that typically goes right into a slush pile.

Are your clients limited to one industry—say, the entertainment field? Do you cater to start-up businesses that may not have a marketing department and approach the CEO directly? Do you work for creative staffing firms, in which case you'd approach a recruiter? Once you know the companies and people in those organizations that you want to target, you can hit them with whatever marketing strategy you'd like.

Also think about the feed, or *pipeline*, of work, you want. Would you rather have a handful of clients providing you a somewhat steady amount of projects? I know freelancers that really only have about two clients, yet are always busy. Do you want to have more of a part-time arrangement with one of your clients where they give you steady assignments? Or do you want every client to use your services once then pass on the word about you? Keep these things in mind as you define the type of workflow you want and the clients that can fulfill those desires.

Who do freelancers work for?

"When it comes to clients, the overwhelming majority of freelancers surveyed (74 percent) go after businesses. However, 17 percent work mainly for individual consumers, 6 percent work for nonprofits, 2 percent pursue government work, and nearly 2 percent focus on associations."

—The 2012 Freelance Industry Report,
www.internationalfreelancersday.com/2012report

For a long time, graphic designer Angela Ferraro-Fanning (*www.1331design.com*) worked with start-ups and other solopreneurs. The work was great, but it was also short-lived. That is, after my fellow Jersey girl created the start-up materials, the clients typically did not need her help anymore, so she had to keep prospecting.

In her case, she sought not to reach a different industry, per se, but to move toward corporate clients with ongoing work. Her goal was to work with medium to large-sized businesses that either had an in-house design or marketing department so she could complement the team, or companies that did not have a designer where she would be the primary creative.

"Deciding this target market shift was one thing; marketing effectively was another," recalls Ferraro-Fanning. She redesigned her logo so it would show her personality yet speak to a corporate-level audience. Next, it was on to her Web site and business collateral. She also went through samples on her Web site to show pieces that were similar to those she wanted to create—a little law of attraction, if you will. In just a few months, she started taking on larger projects consistently.

Who's on Your Hotlist?

When we talk about generating leads, it's a good idea to keep a list or multiple lists of contacts. Don't get too fancy with this; good old Microsoft Excel (or—gasp!—pen and paper) will do. A list will enable you to target and track your efforts, because you may have to reach the same person a few times to engage them.

This *hotlist* is an ever-evolving tool that can ensure you stay on top of your lead generation and marketing efforts. You can certainly generate leads sending off messages and collateral to anyone with an address, but it will probably take much longer because you're going blindly.

You can have multiple lists going, too. I keep a list of existing clients that are likely to use my services again, and also a list of potential clients that includes marketing managers. Because I have done some work editing environmental reports, I also keep a list of contacts in the environmental industry, too.

There are basically two ways to create a hotlist:

1. **Rent a list.** A growing number of companies let you purchase contact information though you usually have to buy a high quantity of leads. Large companies use these services, but you can rent lower-quantity lists.

2. **Create your own list.** You can put either "cold leads" (those who don't know you) or "warm leads" (people that you have some connection with or have interacted with) on your list. Scour your in-box for older project inquiries, rifle through your list of business cards, browse your LinkedIn contacts or members in a social media group, or grab a trade magazine to see if you can track down any key industry players there. You can even hit the Yellow Pages to find businesses that may use your services. These are all smart ways to populate your list.

The list or lists you compile will then serve as the base of recipients for the marketing efforts you choose to take, which we will discuss in the upcoming chapter.

What's your best tip for courting and securing clients?

"The best way to attract the attention of new clients is to consistently meet the deadlines—and exceed the expectations— of current clients. It's true that creative professionals would be wise to market themselves through things like Web sites, email marketing, public appearances, and blogs, but none of these avenues of promotion can compare with word-of-mouth referrals from one exuberant client to a colleague, friend, or neighbor who happens to be looking for creative help for their business or organization."

—Jim Krause, designer/illustrator/photographer/author,
www.jimkrausedesign.com

Using Cold-Calling to Generate Leads

Cold-calling is another way to generate leads, though not all solo-pros are keen on it.

A few years ago, a friend of mine in New Jersey took the plunge into freelancing. Without any formal training in the video arena, John Mitchell (*www.jmitchellproductions.blogspot.com*) decided he wanted to work for himself. Now, my buddy Johnny was always snapping bizarre pictures and shooting humorous videos when we were in college, so you can imagine what I envisioned when he told me he was going into the video business!

I admire Mitchell because his business mindset was simple: He needed clients, so he got them. Leveraging his skills in sales and his beyond-vibrant personality, Mitchell conducted a Google search to identify other videographers in the area and then picked up the phone to see if they needed support. "You could tell who you could connect with and who you couldn't," recalls Mitchell.

He remembers his first client, whom he secured by cold-calling. "[He] and I were just simply shooting the breeze talking like best friends even though we just started talking. We were suddenly talking about camera and editing systems like two friends that knew each other for years," says Mitchell.

I was impressed when Mitchell told me he was so busy with free-lance projects that it was time to go full-time—*and* that he was getting clients by cold-calling! Here was my friend, just starting out, using a method that I dread almost as much as invoicing. Once he began free-lancing full-time, I knew that his business would thrive in no time; he had the personality to get ahead. It was his creative edge!

Cold-calling may not be right for everyone, but if you have a bubbly personality and know how to carry a conversation like my friend here, it's definitely a tactic worth trying.

Here are a few tips to conduct a successful cold call.

Tip #1: Customize Your Message

Cold-calling people on your list is a good idea; chances are when you pick up the phone, you'll already know a little bit about the person because you checked out the company's Web site or the person's LinkedIn profile. Being able to tailor your message is important; you simply have to find something to make it relatable.

"The more customized your message is, the more likely the prospect will be interested in hearing it," Slaunwhite notes.

When you do your research, you'll probably find a nugget of information to incorporate into your call. Perhaps the person on the other end of the line is launching a new product (with which she'll need your assistance in creating the design or copy) or worked with a mutual client of yours (a wonderful conversation-starter!). This type of information helps warm up the tone of the call and engage the prospect.

Tip #2: Don't Be Too Pushy

When you pick up the receiver, don't sound too sales-y or rehearsed—or you could hear a dial tone next.

Slaunwhite says it is vital to speak the way you would normally converse. "Be authentic. Be yourself," Slaunwhite says. "That is, perhaps, the most effective prospecting technique of them all."

That's how Stephanie Jones (*www.cleverfinch.com*), a graphic designer and illustrator from Virginia, has used cold-calling effectively.

She spots companies with approximately 30 to 500 employees that are located within an hour of her and have a marketing director. Then she peeks at their current collateral so she can offer a service they need.

"When I call I am friendly and professional, and I let them know quickly what I do and what I have to offer them," she notes. "I see if they'll discuss any current or upcoming projects that I may be able to help them with and then I send them a link to my portfolio so they can review relevant samples of my work."

Tip #3: Use a Referral

To be honest, I don't do a lot of cold-calling. I have called a few warm leads and was more comfortable that way over calling complete strangers. Maybe you can contact someone you met at an event, know through a mutual colleague, or connected with on LinkedIn. Once you forge a connection and introduce it, the other person is more likely to listen in and not hang up. That can be its own measure of success when you're generating leads on the phone!

Slaunwhite says your chances of success with a cold call will go up greatly if you mention those connections. He says to peruse LinkedIn, or ask clients or colleagues if they know anyone who would be interested in your services.

Tip #4: Prompt a Yes-or-No Response

In another effort not to get dial-toned, your script (if you choose to use one) needs to allow for a pause so the person can tell you upfront if he's not interested. The last thing you want to do is give your name, babble on incessantly like a telemarketer, and not give the recipient a word in edgewise. The prospect may get ticked off and hang up (which *really* sucks if she remembers your name!).

Instead, have an opening statement such as, "Hi, Joe. My name is Kristen Fischer, and your colleague Tom Smith referred me to you. Do you have a moment to speak?"

This lets the person respond so you know if you should go on or let him continue with his day.

How can I get over my cold-call-a-phobia?

"Cold-calling can be a little scary at first but once you realize it's just a voice on another line of the phone it's not that bad.

Honestly, more than half of the calls will be messages on their voice mail anyway so just have a set script and just keep calling...you'll be done with those number of calls in no time. When connecting with people I realize that it's all about being in the right place at the right time, so don't be afraid to make those calls."

—John Mitchell, videographer,
www.jmitchellproductions.blogspot.com

Using E-Mail to Generate Leads

Freelancers rely heavily on e-mail not only for communication with clients; it's a useful method to generate leads, too. If you don't like cold-calling, e-mail can be an awesome way to prospect. It's my favorite!

The concept behind using e-mail to generate leads is quite similar to what we did previously with cold-calling: You are looking to make contact and see if the person is interested in hearing more. You're not really going for the "whole sell" when you use e-mail to prospect. You're sending a message to a lead you have targeted to see if she bites. If so, *then* you can sell.

There are seven aspects that, when used properly, can help you engage leads:

1. **Find the right recipient.** We talked about targeting leads that will be most beneficial. That's why you must have the name and e-mail address of the recipient who will receive your message.

2. **Create a killer subject line.** It only takes a few words to entice the recipient to open your message, and the best way to do that is to include their first or first and last name in the subject line to show you're not a spambot. You can also put in the name of the company. Words such as *help, reminder, percent off, free,* and *discount*—not to mention writing in all caps—may alert a spam box, so steer clear of

those. I like to include the name of the recipient and the word *copywriting,* because the leads I target already know what copywriting is and likely use contractors.

3. **Add an introduction.** Remember: You want to entice the recipient to read your message, so create a short introductory paragraph that states your name and what you *have to offer.* I like to tell prospects I am a copywriter available if the company needs press releases, brochures, or Web site content.

4. **Request action.** Here's where you ask if the recipient is the appropriate person to contact about your services, and if not, ask if he can connect you with the right person. Otherwise, the recipient may not consider passing it along to the correct person; he may just hit "delete." You also want to let the recipient know he should contact you if he is interested.

5. **Share your deets.** Include a signature with your phone number, e-mail, and Web site address; mine displays my mailing address as well. These details make it easy for the recipient to contact you or pass your information along with everything she needs.

6. **Encourage future connections.** Sometimes I include a sentence in the message to encourage the recipient to hold on to my contact information if he needs it in the future. That has been helpful, too, because then the recipient who doesn't need your services at the time may be more apt to hang on to it and contact you in the future.

7. **Follow up if you want.** If I do not hear back in about a week, I don't always follow up with a "Did you get my e-mail?" message because I generally find them annoying. That said, you can follow up if you'd like, so long as you give the recipient a few days. Beyond that, you can choose to approach the potential lead another time, or move on to new prospects.

Again, this is a beneficial way to make connections, which drive many freelancers' businesses. Once you have a lead, you can approach him or her with more information about your services. Send the prospect a brochure or add him or her to your e-mail list. That person is familiar with you now, and not a stranger; you've got a warm lead. Even if you don't receive a project right away, it can still be a valuable connection.

Other Ways to Sniff Out the Bacon

I recently spoke with a friend who lost her job and sought assistance with her resume. She claimed she had sent out two resumes and had run out of options. I kind of balked, because there were plenty of places she could send it to, but she was in the "apply to open positions only" mindset.

Although that can be very valuable for full-time professionals looking for 9-to-5 jobs, the recession seems to have introduced more of a proactive concept that encourages job-seekers to make their own job opportunities by approaching employers with their skills instead of waiting for an open position. This is the kind of mindset that solo-pros have relied on for years, and now the rest of the world seems to be catching on—finally!

That said, there are some more traditional ways to find projects. You can use job boards; some companies list their needs for freelancers and part-time gigs on popular job Web sites such as *www.monster.com*. You may choose to work on government contracts, which can be a logical progression if you have a background in that arena. Additionally, taking jobs through creative staffing firms can provide solid opportunities to keep a steady paycheck coming in while you build your biz.

Job-Hunting

Another way to find work is to look at job boards, newspapers, or explore bidding Web sites such as *www.elance.com*. Explore what avenues work for *you*, because you never know where your next gig comes from. A mix of job-searching and targeting leads—as well as receiving referrals—has worked well for me.

Stephanie Jones (*www.cleverfinch.com*), a graphic designer and illustrator from Virginia, used bidding Web sites to find design gigs when she started freelancing, but quickly decided the Web sites were not worth her time. "They provide so much competition that the client wields enormous power," she says.

Web sites like *www.monster.com* and *www.careerbuilder.com* can offer unmined opportunities for jobs—and leads. To spot a lead, look at the bottom of an ad and get the name, phone number, or e-mail of a contact and—*presto-chango!*—there's a possible lead. You can then contact the person to see if she is interested in your services. If the human resources liaison is listed, ask if he handles freelancers or request the marketing director's information. It's an indirect way of finding leads, but it can be quite effective.

What are some other methods I can use to find clients and projects?

"According to the 2012 Freelance Industry Report, 23.8 percent of freelancers relied on referrals and 23.8 percent used word-of-mouth. Personal and professional networks account for how 16.9 percent of freelancers nabbed jobs; while 6.3 percent used online job boards, 6.2 percent utilized networking, 2.8 percent used social media, 1.8 percent use paid directories, and just 1.7 percent used cold-calling. Other methods include search engine optimization, direct mail, Craigslist.com, blogging, newsletters, books, public speaking, and article marketing."

—*The 2012 Freelance Industry Report,*
www.internationalfreelancersday.com/2012report

Working for the Government

Local, state, and federal governments can be a useful—not to mention lucrative—source of project work. I have never worked for a government agency directly, but I have worked for government contractors. This sector isn't prominently mentioned as a main source of income for freelancers, but I'm not sure why because the paychecks can be so attractive and the work can be steady. I think this route isn't as popular because it involves a bit of a procedure.

The process includes:

→ **Obtain a Dun & Bradstreet D-U-N-S® Number.** This is a must for federal contract work. It's good to have in general if you work in the government sector.

→ **Register with the Central Contractor Registration (CCR) and the System of Award Management (SAM).** These are the leading databases that government entities go to when looking for vendors and contractors.

→ **Register in ORCA.** Fill out the solicitation clauses and certifications in the Online Representations and Certifications Application (ORCA), which verifies information on your company.

→ **Get a Past Performance Evaluation from Open Ratings** *(www.openratings.com).* This verifies that you are a legitimate professional.

→ **Obtain a North American Industry Classification System (NAICS) code.** This may be necessary for clerical and tax purposes.

You may need to hold business insurance depending on the job and the state you live in. Check out some resources (your local library may be a great place to start) to learn more about securing government contracts. Most of the people I know that get them are never scraping for more clients.

Resource
Visit *www.sba.gov/content/register-government-contracting* and *www. freelancewrite.about.com/od/freelancejobresources/ss/fedcontr.htm* **to find out more about how to become a government contractor. Check out FedBizOpps at** *www.fbo.gov* **for a database of opportunities.**

Working for Creative Staffing Firms

In addition to working for marketing agencies, creative agencies (or creative staffing firms) offer viable job opportunities. They tend to hire more part- and full-time professionals with some gigs leading to full-time work, but many of them offer freelance projects, too.

Companies hire creative staffing firms to fulfill their talent needs. You may have heard of some of the big ones, such as Aquent, The Creative Group, Artisan, and Creative Circle.

To work with a creative staffing firm, begin by looking at some of the jobs they offer, which will be on their own Web sites and on general job boards. Most of the work is on-site, and a lot of the big agencies are located in and around major cities.

Companies retain creative agencies to "screen" candidates. They ultimately can approve or reject you for the job, but the recruiter liaises between you and the company so you don't have to do a lot of that back-and-forth. All you need to do to get started is register. The agency may want to meet you or request you take a test so they can assess your abilities. They're probably going to want a resume, too; even creatives need them!

What are some no-no's when you're working on site for a client?

"Some are quite obvious: Don't show up late, don't be overly casual in your dress or speech, and don't be a jerk! Based on my experiences, don't assume you can wear headphones; ask first, even if you see everyone rocking out in their own personal disco. Don't wear anything too quirky that might earn you a nickname. Don't blog from work, or if you must, change the timestamp on the post in case someone finds your blog, which they will. Don't mention where you're working on social media sites and especially don't mention what projects you're working on."

—Prescott Perez-Fox, art director/graphic designer, *www.strshp.com*

Prescott Perez-Fox (*www.strshp.com*), an art director and graphic designer from New Jersey, says working for a creative agency can be very lucrative, and there are certainly advantages. "A multi-week job, with 40+ hours a week, can definitely provide a nice bump to your bank account and give you a bit of breathing room for when work slows down," he notes.

It also gives you exposure to build up a network—another benefit if you're just starting out. Because big companies typically retain agencies and never solicit freelancers, it also gives you access to work for a well-known brand. Hopefully, the projects you work on can go in your portfolio, depending on what the contract stipulates.

Some people who have used agencies to secure freelance gigs have wound up going back to a full-time job as a result of taking a short-term gig. This can happen if the company that retained the agency wants to hire the freelancer directly. In some cases, it's a plus; you may freelance and decide it's not for you. But if you want to stay as a solo-pro, stick to short-term gigs from staffing firms.

As with everything, there are some downsides to working at a creative agency. "You'll find that you might go six months, work for half a dozen different firms, and come away with maybe one project in your book," Perez-Fox says. In his experience, not many clients let him put samples of work he has created for them on his Web site.

Another disadvantage is that creative agencies typically only hire for production, so you will not have much of a say in projects unless you have a gig on the management level. (Most companies keep creative managers employed full-time and do not use creative agencies to find them.)

To top it off, even though you may be surrounded by people, it can be lonely. "Working short-term jobs can make it seems like it's always your first day," Perez-Fox notes.

I like the concept of being open to agencies, expressly as you start out as a freelancer. It's a useful way to keep money coming in while you build your client roster.

Sweet Success
Good Timing

A few years back, writer David Geer (*www.davidgeer.com*) approached the editor of a Web site he liked. He connected with the editor, who did not hire him, yet the two stayed in touch.

"I don't remember ever asking him to point me to anyone," recalls Geer, who resides in Ohio. "I simply took a genuine interest in who he was and he did likewise."

One day, Geer's acquaintance e-mailed him to say that a friend of his at a mid-sized company in the technology industry was looking for writers. He wanted to know if Geer would like to be introduced to this friend.

As a result of the partnership, Geer scored months of work and several thousand dollars in revenue. Though Geer had never worked for his e-mail buddy, the acquaintance trusted him to work for his friend—and the connection paid off!

"If you build relationships, patiently focusing on the people who may be able to recommend you some day, some of these relationships will bear fruit," says Geer.

Beginner Mishap
Adding Insult to Copy

When Angela Ferraro-Fanning (*www.1331design.com*), a graphic designer from New Jersey, moved to a new city and started her full-time freelance business, she decided to single out clients she wanted to work for—such as salons and restaurants—that she thought could use design help.

She then drafted what she called a "cold-call-style" letter saying how much she liked the business and that she thought their branding and design deserved a higher level of visual appeal. "At the time, I thought I was being slightly bold and honest. I thought I was opening up a conversation. The result? No calls," Ferraro-Fanning says. "I basically presented myself by insulting the prospect." Although many freelancers have taken a similar approach (some with more favorable results), Ferraro-Fanning says the move was probably a poor way to introduce her business.

Years later, she made her way in to some of the restaurants she formerly had targeted. "I'd see the owner walking around and wonder, 'Does she know who I am? Does she remember that letter I sent her?' I hope not."

"To this day I still regret trying to gain clients this way," confesses Ferraro-Fanning.

Chapter 6

Talking Up Your Talent

Now that you have some solid leads to target, it's time to start spreading the word about your services. Part of marketing involves approaching prospects and converting them into clients; the other part involves less direct methods that will strengthen your platform as a professional, lending you the kind of credibility that attracts clients to you.

No matter how good you get at what you do, or how many referrals you receive, it's a good idea to continue marketing your services on an ongoing basis. Through time, you may not have to put so much effort into marketing because you will have a solid client base and an influx of projects from referrals. I like to remember, though, that clients aren't permanent, so you always need to be ready to obtain new ones at a moment's notice in order to stay in business.

What Are Your Marketing Goals?

I like to put some thought into the different marketing tactics I use. There could be more than just one, and there probably should be. For example, I use promotional strategies to boost my overall credibility and image, but also to promote myself to leads.

One of my marketing goals is to secure work with companies that will give me projects on an ongoing basis, providing a feed of work. Another objective is to garner glowing testimonials and referrals. You may also want to get more experience to build up your portfolio of clips, which, in turn, generates more leads and builds your brand.

A lot of rookies tend to focus solely on securing projects, and I understand that mentality because, well, bills need to be paid! Remember as you go along in your career not to ignore existing clients; even if they don't use your services regularly (or ever again), they may refer you to someone else who can send on work. Existing and past clients are a valuable demographic that you'll want to keep on your hotlist.

Using Your Creative Edge to Win at Marketing

When you establish your marketing goals, be sure to remember the most important ingredient of success: yourself. Your creative edge has a lot to do with how effective your marketing efforts can be. For example, if you're a better writer than speaker, cold-calling may not be your best bet. That's okay; use an e-mail newsletter instead.

So much of what we hear when we look for useful information to run our businesses is "cookie cutterish." It's "Do this..." or "Follow steps one, two, three...."

Screw the steps, guys.

When you're filing taxes you need to follow rules and instructions, but when it comes to marketing you have more flexibility. Whatever you want to do, give it a shot. The worst that can happen is that it doesn't work and you try another method.

Luckily, you have your inner compass to guide you. That is, you know what you're good at. Use your writing abilities if that's your forte. Leverage your love of gabbing to form relationships. Put your artistic skills to work for a cool Web site or business card. Those are the types of skills that can give you a competitive edge; you simply have to embrace them.

Making a Budget

Before you launch your dream marketing campaign, you'll want to think about costs. Trust me: It's easy to get carried away when you see some of the cool things you can use to market yourself, so it's important to curb your spending—especially until you know what works.

This all depends on *how* you want to market yourself. The avenues you use all have different costs associated with them; some are more affordable than others.

Take e-mail marketing. I'm a huge advocate of using the Internet to promote myself. When I began business, I would write short e-mails telling prospective clients about myself, my specialties, and what I could do for them. Aside from the time it took to craft and send the messages, it was virtually free.

E-mail marketing continues to be most effective for me, and I think a huge reason is because writing is one of my natural talents. Have some sort of budget in mind, but don't make it a huge production. Just jot down some numbers and make sure you have the cash to cover your expenses.

Personally, I think bringing in a model like that can be confusing and could turn you off from marketing altogether. So until you get the hang of it, start with a simple budget (even $100 can work) and stick to a target list of maybe 50 or 100 leads.

Just to give you an idea, my postcard campaigns usually go out to about 50 people at a time. When I send out a 4" x 6" postcard, I pay about $35 for 100 postcards. Postcard stamps at the time of this writing were 29 cents. So to print and send all of them, I am looking at spending 64 cents per postcard, or $64. Pretty cheap, right? If I get just one project out of it, it has more than paid for itself. Usually, I accept a call from an existing client or prospective customer that says the card came at the perfect time—they've got a project they need to start next week. That's what I call ideal.

There *are* plenty of models to help you determine the exact return on investment. My take? Don't take a huge financial risk with your marketing so you don't waste your time analyzing it! Start small, see what works, and then see what you want to do next. If one method continues to work well for you, stick to it and don't rule out other approaches as time goes on. Keep the math simple to see how much your marketing efforts yield.

As your business has grown, have you had to market as much?

"In the beginning I was just happy to work for anyone that would hire me, but soon enough I realized I had to take control of my marketing, so some source book advertising in The Arizona Portfolio, Black Book, Creativa; and of course direct mail post cards to a mailing list I created, but frankly database management can be a full-time job, so services like Agency Access is great for keeping in contact."

—Dan Coogan, photographer, *www.cooganphoto.com*

Bust Out Your Marketing Toolbox

According to the 2012 Freelance Industry Report, solo-pros say finding clients is their biggest challenge. Why is it, then, that nearly 53 percent of them spend less than five hours per month on self-promotion?

After you have generated leads, there are five active ways to get the word out: marketing collateral, e-mail marketing, public relations, social media, and networking. Each can be used to generate leads, and each can be used with existing clients or prospects to land more work and build your street cred.

Marketing Tool #1: Print Marketing Collateral

The thought of sending out a brochure may sound a little "old school," but the tactic can be very effective. From time to time, I still send out a postcard or brochure. Print collateral is also a nice way to follow up with prospects so they have a tangible reminder of who you are and what you have to offer.

Marketing collateral is good for reaching the type of folks that prefer to have something in hand. That way, the next time a prospect needs someone with your expertise, your trusty brochure is front and center.

Marketing collateral can take a few mailings, months, or years to yield results, but most solo-pros agree it is a valuable tactic. A print campaign doesn't need to be done monthly. In fact, you can probably get away with doing one a few times a year.

Try to be practical when it comes to collateral, because you have to purchase the materials to create it, design it, and then mail it. For example, how large is the piece you want to mail? Will it fit in a standard envelope, and if not, how much will appropriate envelopes cost? What will the mailing cost be? Can a standard stamp cover it? Can you save more money by having your hometown printer produce it, can you print it yourself, or should you look at on-line printing operations? These are all factors to put into a budget.

Resource
Check out *nextdayflyers.com, www.jakprints.com, www.psprint. com,* **or** *www.vistaprint.com.*

Marketing Tool #2: E-Mail Marketing

So there's the old-school marketing manager or art director who likes print collateral, but there are also plenty of leads that like everything digital—including your pitch. Even though your message arrives electronically, it's still collateral, so it still needs to promote you well.

There are two forms of what I consider as e-mail marketing: sending inquiries via e-mail and sending an e-mail newsletter. Let's take a look at how these marketing strategies can help you convert leads into clients.

The Marketing E-Mail

This form of marketing is almost second nature for most of us—so much that we may not realize it's a proven marketing technique. Before I went full-time as a freelancer, I sent out casual e-mails to introduce myself to prospects. It seemed logical—not to mention economical—to say, "Here's what I can do for you. Let me know if you are interested." We talked about putting together this type of message in the previous chapter, so you should be familiar with what goes into a good prospecting message. Other than that, it's all about timing.

I consider myself to have some pretty amazing powers when it comes to using e-mail for marketing. With almost every campaign I send, I receive at least one response back saying something like, "I was just talking to my colleague about hiring a copywriter. When can we meet?"

Realistically, you will not get a response from every e-mail you send. In fact, the majority of e-mails I send go off into a cyberspace void. That's okay. The ones who respond are the people looking for your services.

The E-Mail Newsletter

This strategy can help you land clients, but it's more about giving something of value to prospects and existing clients. You're not just saying, "I need to pay my rent this month. Have any assignments for me?" Instead, you are sharing your expertise with at least one article that gives the recipients some value based on your specialty. They pick up on the value and think of you next time they need your services. In my newsletter, I like to offer writing tips, for example.

Publishing a newsletter is a wonderful way to highlight what you have been up to lately. I find clients think it's cool to hear that I write books on the side, or am published in magazines they read. Sharing this information can be priceless, because you never know when they will relate to something you mention and contact you. Some may see an article you put together and pass it on to a colleague because they think the other person can use that information—and there you are in front of another prospect that was never even on your hotlist.

One more plus about e-mail newsletters: They make you look good. They show you're into your profession and build authority. Perhaps a client who gave you work years ago wasn't sure if you were the person to take on a new job, but then he sees that you have just published an impressive e-book and decides to give you a shot.

Resource

Popular e-mail marketing tools include *www.mailchimp.com*, *www.godaddy.com*, *www.icontact.com*, *www.aweber.com*, *www.verticalresponse.com*, and *www.constantcontact.com*.

Marketing Tool #3: Public Relations

Once you have something newsworthy to share with others, it can be in your best interest to do just that. It builds integrity, not to mention gives you a reason to blast out another e-mail newsletter when you thought you had nothing to write about. With something newsworthy, now you do.

After I published *Creatively Self-Employed,* I put out press releases to newspapers and news organizations. The local ones seemed to respond more readily than the nationals, especially because my book was self-published. Those press releases got attention, and a few publications interviewed me for a feature on local authors. That also got the word out that I was a copywriter, which was awesome for business.

Even if I didn't get a call for work out of it, I put the clipping in a section of my Web site devoted to press—a section that publicity pros check out when they are deciding if they should feature you.

When I received my certification in resume writing, I let the local papers know by sending a press release. If you are chosen to speak at an event or conference, tell your newspaper about it. A competent image is another aspect of marketing that, as I said, can help you nab clients. When they see how credible you are, it can influence them to call.

I like to think of public relations as an "indirect" marketing technique. As you can tell from my own experiences, it is certainly one that can be very useful to cultivate your business.

I can hear the nay-saying already: "I don't want to be in the spotlight." "Sending out press releases about myself sounds so arrogant, doesn't it?" This is a pretty common sentiment from most creative freelancers. Because your business is you, you have to promote yourself as an individual and a brand. That's what huge corporations do. In fact, they have large marketing departments devoted to things such as creating collateral, securing mentions in the media, and managing their brand.

Marketing—and PR in particular—isn't about bragging. It's about doing business. I'm not saying to jump on every possible press opportunity, but you have to work up to some comfort level in promoting your business and seize opportunities when they arise. The truth is, no matter how talented you are, you are not likely to be able to sustain a profitable business if you are not willing to promote it.

Must-Read
The New Rules of Marketing & PR: How to Use Social Media, Online Video, Mobile Applications, Blogs, News Releases, and Viral Marketing to Reach Buyers Directly by **David Meerman Scott**

Why do creative professionals need to work on public relations?

"I try to put at least a minimal amount of effort into self-promotion and public relations. Most of my self-promotion is done through my Web site and word-of-mouth. My public relations program can be summed up in one word: yes. For example, when I'm asked to speak to a group of business people or students about design, I like to answer with a big, fat 'yes'; and when a friend needs a first-class logo designed for their save-the-world start-up business (without having the means to pay for it), I say 'yes.' Saying yes is probably a much better karma-booster than saying no, and it can also lead to business-boosting exposure."

—Jim Krause, designer/illustrator/photographer/author,
www.jimkrausedesign.com

How to Write a Press Release

I know that many creative professionals do not enjoy the writing process, but press releases are a standard tool in the business world; you should familiarize yourself with them.

A press release announces something newsworthy and timely. For example, if you provide Web site design, sending out a press release to the newspaper telling them about your artistic talent isn't going to get picked up. If you recently launched a Web site for a company that enables consumers to purchase items online, your crafts got picked up for a television show, or you won a design contest, those would be newsworthy examples.

The following are five major components to writing an excellent press release:

1. **The headline.** Take a look at news headlines to get a feel for the style of writing. Think in terms of action when you write. Instead of *"Ramen Noodles, Rent and Resumes Book Released,"* you can see how "Local Author to Host Book Signing for Latest Book on Post-Collegiate Life" is more effective. It gives the news upfront and points to an event or something timely; *that's the newsworthy part.* You can also create a sub-headline to give more detail and draw people to read on.

2. **The lead paragraph.** Reiterate the news upfront, stating what the news is, exactly. Cover the who, what, when, where, and why.

3. **The quote.** Break up the prose with a quote. It offers a personal touch, and gives you the opportunity to speak clearly and put a voice to the name of your business. When I wrote a press release to announce my book signing, I mentioned how grateful I was to the local bookstore for hosting the event.

4. **The boilerplate.** The last paragraph is always a short biography with a link to your Web site.

5. **Contact information.** Put your contact information prominently on the press release. If a member of the press is interested in writing a story on the press release, or maybe just rewriting it into a blurb, they can easily contact you to confirm any details.

Media Relations

Another way to use PR is to offer quotes to reporters looking for them, so you are sharing your expertise and positioning yourself as an expert. To do this, you have to go to the places where reporters scout out sources so you can respond to their inquiries and be featured in their stories and books. If you visit *www.helpareporter.com,* you can sign up for free daily leads from reporters. This tool, otherwise known as HARO (Help a Reporter Out), has been instrumental to assist me in promoting myself and my books—and it doesn't cost a thing!

Remember when you pitch a reporter to offer something useful. Don't just say, "I have a great story for your article. Call me!" Journalists hear a million requests like that. Instead, offer an enticing tip or offer to be interviewed. This is another fantastic way to get your name out there. It shows that you are a prominent leader in your field—and if nothing else, gives you something newsworthy to add to your e-mail newsletter!

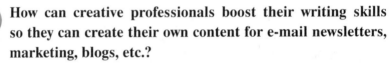 **How can creative professionals boost their writing skills so they can create their own content for e-mail newsletters, marketing, blogs, etc.?**

"Read. Read lots. Why? Because people who regularly read develop an inner ear that is capable of hearing the sound, construction and rhythm of good writing—whether the writing comes from within or without."

—Jim Krause, designer/illustrator/photographer/author, *www.jimkrausedesign.com*

Marketing Tool #4: Social Media

Social media is growing in popularity and can be a useful tool to not only land gigs; it can serve as a useful platform for solo-pros looking to build a professional standing and establish themselves as competent leaders. Twitter and LinkedIn, especially, have been very helpful for my business. Plenty of creative professionals use those along with Facebook (and others) to promote themselves, meet other freelancers, and connect with prospective clients. (For me, Facebook is solely for personal use.)

Sarah Griffin, who works as a chemist in Kansas by day and runs *www.secretsivenevertold.com* on the side, said Facebook has been instrumental to generate publicity for her Web site and book. "I use Facebook to communicate with my followers daily. Offering specials and deals for your Facebook fans is a great way to get more fans, which is more people who you will be able to have constant contact with. Social media is where it's at," Griffin says.

Agreed, Sarah. Solo-pros just need to make sure they are using the tool effectively and professionally. By now, we all know not to rat out rude clients by name. For those of us who sometimes vent via Twitter, it may not always be the best idea though it can be a way to connect with others.

You'll find plenty of material on-line about how freelancers can use these social networks professionally. When you create an account, think about what type of connection you want to make. For instance, I use LinkedIn to connect with prospects, obtain testimonials, and get specific contact information to pitch magazine editors. I like the groups, too, and have been able to find sources for when I am working on a story.

Using Twitter

Whereas LinkedIn is more of a business tool, Twitter doesn't necessarily have to be used for business. It can, however, be a very powerful tool if used correctly. I use it more to cultivate relationships with colleagues and fellow creatives. For example, after you meet someone at a conference or event, you can add him or her to your LinkedIn network and then send a tweet saying it was nice to meet her to reinforce the connection. I know freelancers that have tweeted others before an event, which paved the way for a smoother introduction when they met face-to-face.

I like to put a mix of tweets about everyday life along with links to articles I have written that offer value to colleagues *and* clients. It's another tool to help me secure sources for interviews when I am writing a piece for a magazine.

If you follow my tweets, I know—I talk way too much about football! But that's the kind of thing that has enabled me to connect with others on a more personal level. That's why I don't stick to only self-promotional tweets.

Twitter's also a rockin' tool to use to support fellow creatives as well as colleagues. I love the support I've gotten from other freelancers using it, and it's always nice to give a shout-out to a client to show you are thinking of them.

Marketing Tool #5: Networking

When I first launched my business, I attended some networking events. At the time, I knew to network but didn't realize how valuable it was to establish a goal in networking or see if the groups I was interested in were the right match for my needs. At the time, that was to drum up clients.

Networking groups can help you generate leads, and are also a goldmine if you're a social butterfly stuck working home alone. In addition to getting you out of the office a little bit, they are an ideal avenue to exchange ideas, receive support, and meet prospective clients—or people who know them.

I once attended an event a well-known group of creative professionals in my area. I worked the room and doled out some business cards, heard a speaker, and ate lunch. I left with a bunch of business cards, mostly from other writers. That would have been perfect if I wanted to hire another writer or connect with other writers for *support,* but I was looking for *leads.* Sure, I can get work from other writers who may farm out their overflow, but I would stand a better chance to secure the type of ongoing work I wanted from my own clients if I met them directly.

After that, I gave up on networking, at least for a while. Until I realized I was doing it all wrong! Find out a little about the groups you are interested in and who the members are. If you want to meet other creatives, a group of artists is perfect. But if you're looking for leads, try a group with people in other roles that *need your services,* such as creative directors, executives, and managers—the types of professionals in a multi-disciplinary networking group can use the marketing collateral that so many solo-pros develop, so reaching out to them would be a smart idea for a copywriter or Web site developer. If you licensed designs or illustrations, it may be a good idea to attend an industry trade show with prospects that are looking for artwork.

Be on the lookout for networking opportunities, but also pay attention to the costs involved. Town chambers of commerce can be very useful but often come with a yearly fee. Also, many organizations have meetings involving food, and that can cost you every time you attend. Instead, you may want to try to get a feel for some low-cost or free events first. Some groups you will mesh with; others you may not. Explore all of your options to find a group (or groups) that works for you.

Last year, I attended a meeting for a group of creative professionals and went solely because I wanted to connect with others in my field. I didn't go expecting work out of it. I came out with some good, local connections I still touch base with. I'm eager to attend similar events in the future.

Massachusetts-based freelance writer Susan Johnston (*www.susan-johnston.com*) says that it takes time to see the positive effects that can come from networking. "A lot of people expect networking to have an immediate effect, but it takes time to see the results of those interactions, so it's more of a long-term strategy. Even if I don't leave an event with the business card of someone who's likely to hire me, I can appreciate the fact that the event got me out of my apartment and gave me practice at networking with others in the industry," she says.

I'm going to a networking event. What can I expect?

"Bring a plethora of business cards. You will need them. Don't be surprised if you're asked to introduce yourself to the group and briefly describe the services you offer. It's also a good idea to send a 'so nice to have met you' e-mail to each person who gave you a business card."

—Amber Timmerman, graphic designer/Web designer,
www.mintyfreshdesign.com

So there you have it: five actionable strategies that you can use to get the word out about your services. In addition to the action steps, having a platform in place to funnel leads to is key. For example, when you send out a direct mail piece or an e-mail newsletter, you want people to contact you, so you would include your phone number and Web site address.

Your Web site is kind of a landing space for most prospects, because they usually like to check you out before they call. They want to know which clients you have worked with and see samples of what you have done. That's why having an awesome Web site is so important.

We touched on this in Chapter 2, but it seems fitting to include more information on the importance of your Web site. You can't shove it in front of prospects' faces, but when they are interested in your services or products, you can be sure it's the first place they'll look. From its design and functionality to wording and content, your Web site has to be phenomenal.

Bryn Mooth, a freelance writer based in Cincinnati, used designer Jill Anderson (*www.jilllynndesign.com*) to create her masterpiece at *www. brynmooth.com*. I like her Web site because it visually conveys her brand and was built around her specialties in the food, health, and design arenas.

Mooth says it took her a while to realize that her original recipe blog wasn't representing what she had to offer. She says Anderson's design is professional and feels very authentic with regards to who she is as both a person and a professional. "The type, color scheme and 'linen-look' background of my site has a sort of organic, homey appeal, and it reflects the honest, personal approach in my writing," Mooth says, referencing her current Web site.

Letting your personality shine through is important. Keep in mind that the Web site doesn't have to be flashy; something simple works as long as it looks authentic and neat. It's going to be the hub where you put all the testimonials you work so hard for as well as your press clippings—and so much more. Make it good!

 Must-Read
Creative Girl: The Ultimate Guide for Turning Talent and Creativity into a Real Career by **Katharine Sise**

The Creative Professional's Resume

Why on Earth is there a section about resumes in this book, you may ask? Because I find that many solo-pros think they are exempt from having one!

"I don't need a resume. I'm not 'corporate' anymore. I'm an 'indie' now," you may say. Or you may not have much of a background in the field of your creative talent and think your resume could wind up empty.

Newsflash: It doesn't matter. You still need a resume.

Why? That's twofold. First, no matter how independent of an independent contractor you are, you'll need to do business, and that will likely happen with other companies. If you want to earn money from that world, you have to speak their language—or at least show you know it on paper—and you do that with a resume. Having a Web site is *not* enough!

The other reason to have a resume when you have no intention of getting near a cubicle again is because it is a *fantastic* basis for your marketing platform. Think about it: You send out postcards or an e-mail newsletter to get clients. They visit your Web site, which has the standard page about you and a listing of your services. Without a resume on your Web site, you are alienating the prospect that comes to your page and wants to go directly to a document to find out what your background is. Clips are great, but the traditional hiring model relies on resumes, so your marketing efforts could go to waste if you don't appeal to that crowd, too.

Resumes may not apply to artisans who sell products as much as they do to other types of creatives that provide services. Still, you should have one. If you want to obtain creative freelance projects, they are likely handled by a company's art or marketing department. These departments are parts of companies, so again, speaking their language is critical. Even if the art director is laid-back about hiring contractors, he may still need a resume to include in your hiring paperwork.

Sadly, some creative professionals are so anti-corporate (rightfully so, they've may have been burned by a company or detested the corporate lifestyle enough to start a solo biz) that they never accept how important it is to have a resume and therefore do not create one. You could be the most talented person in your field, but if you don't have a resume, you may not be able to apply for the job you want.

Your resume does not have to go on your Web site; if you post it or not, that's up to you. But *do* come up with a resume and have it on hand. Nothing is worse than losing an amazing job opportunity because you didn't have a resume to submit.

To help you create a resume, here are three tips to keep in mind.

Tip #1: Objective vs. Profile

The first thing other than the design of your resume that will likely grab attention is what comes first. In the past, it was a once-sentence objective, but times have changed. Nowadays, you only use an objective if you're fresh out of college or just entering the workforce. I think most people reading this book have had some professional experience, even if it is not in the creative field they are pursuing. In that case, a profile is a better choice than an objective.

What's the difference between a profile and an objective, you may ask? The profile gives a summary of your skills and what you have to offer, whereas the objective states what you want to do, or your goal.

When you set out to create your profile, really think about what message you want to get across. Jot down some notes before you try to come up with fancy wording, then draft three to seven sentences to create your profile. Browse sample resumes on-line to get an idea of phrases or words you like, or visit my Web site (*www.kristenfischer.com*) to take a peek at my resume.

Tip #2: Focus on Accomplishments—Not Just Responsibilities

A lot of the resumes I see floating out there typically include a list of bullets that only offer a glimpse into what a person has done. Instead, I recommend breaking up each job into duties *and* accomplishments so you show not only what you did on a typical day, but how you excelled at it and the results you achieved.

Most people I write resumes for do not believe they have anything worth writing about, but when you think of your experiences, consider small things such as "delivered consistently excellent customer service" or "implemented a new system." Any way you can show how *you* went above and beyond speaks volumes about what you can do, especially as a solopreneur.

Tip #3: Use the Right Language

You don't have to be a pro resume writer to produce a knockout document. Write from a third-person perspective. Jazz up the wording with some verbs and industry buzzwords. Even if you worked formerly as a receptionist answering phones, you could state something like "Responded to client phone inquiries." See how the right words elevate the tone of the document?

Add specific terms to show the breadth of your expertise. In my resume, I don't just state that I am a copywriter; I include the types of services I have to offer, such as creating Web site content, brochures, and press releases. I add industry terms such as *media relations* and *branding.*

Finally, start statements in the section on personal experience with an action verb, and don't repeat the same word.

As you can tell, how you represent yourself is a vital component of your overall marketing efforts. In the sea of freelancers, "looks"—at least how you project yourself and what you have to offer—mean everything. Even if you work in grungy jeans and t-shirts covered in paint every day, make sure your resume sparkles.

How can I get my work out there so people can get a feel for my visual aesthetic and my unique sense of style?

"The best way that I've been able to get my work out there is through my Web site—contacting people and sending a sample image or two along with the link. I like using HTML e-mail templates, too, such as MailChimp. I've also entered call for entries for exhibits, online, and through galleries."

—Carey Kirkella, lifestyle/portrait photographer,
www.careykirkella.com

Sweet Success
Webbing Clients With Your Web Site

Head over to *www.aubreandrus.com* so you can see the power that comes with having a fantastic Web site. Aubre Andrus, a Seattle-based writer, says that launching her Web site was instrumental to her success as a solo-pro. "It was actually amazing how relieved and 'official' I felt once the site went up," recalls Andrus, who retained a former coworker to design it and let a friend's younger brother program the Web site. They created the comic-inspired motif with bold colors that makes Andrus's Web site such a distinctive delight. "The Web site has gotten tons of compliments and it helps me stand out from the competition. It's a super-creative design—not your typical, boring writing Web site—but most importantly, it shows off my portfolio, blog, and social media presences," says Andrus.

"Meanwhile, my matching business cards—although adorable—are collecting dust in my desk drawer," she notes. "I only pass them out to other writers I meet at conferences."

Beginner Mishap
Missing the Target

When Amy Philip (*www.careercertain.com*), a leadership career consultant and resume writer from Brooklyn, decided to launch her business, she figured a broad range of services would work best. She created a Web site, logo, messaging, and overall brand to reflect herself. "Big mistake. It's not about me—it's about the customer," notes Philip. "I believed that I needed to be open and willing to take on whatever type of work came my way. I didn't quite see and appreciate the full value of specialization."

Philip then asked herself what kind of messaging, look, and feel she wanted to project through her brand and collateral. Then she aligned her marketing strategy with the branding message and marketing collateral to better target the types of clients she wants—and those she can provide the best value to. "If what you do doesn't speak to and resonate with your target client, it's not going to work and it will attract the wrong type of client and confuse the client you are trying to attract," she says.

"I can't be all things to all people...the more targeted you can be the better," Philip says. "This translates into everything you do for your business—from the content of your on-line marketing to the tone of your messaging and blog posts you write...everything you do needs to speak to your target client base."

Chapter 7

Connecting With Clients

Whether you provide a one-time service or take on multiple projects for a client, freelancers must be as diligent in client relations as they are talented in their craft.

Welcome to another aspect of business: customer service. A lot of freelancers tend to use the term *client relations* more because they refer to their customers as clients. However you refer to your clients, the partnership you form with them—and the service you provide—speaks volumes about your business and your brand. It differentiates you from the bazillion other contractors out there. And if you draw upon your creative edge, you can really stand out from a crowd, because we all have something unique to offer.

Though you can deliver great service without forging much of a customer relationship, I tend to think that developing a strong rapport with clients is an integral part of delivering fantastic customer service. Some freelancers believe the only way to go "above and beyond" for clients is to include extra services or add on a freebie as part of the project; the truth is, there are many other ways to cultivate stronger client relations and provide exceptional customer service.

According to the 2012 Freelance Industry Report, 46 percent of freelancers tend to work for a single client for a year or longer, and 30 percent say they teamed up with the same client for more than two years. You don't just contract more work solely by being talented; the way you treat clients is an important factor and a definite link to your success as a solo-pro. If you're like me and enjoy repeat work from cool clients, these relationships are quite significant.

Courting Clients

If you thought customer service was just something you got in a store, think again. You're in business now, and you have to provide it, too. (That doesn't mean you have to let people walk all over you, though. We'll go there in Chapter 8.)

I acquired customer service skills at my first job as a sales associate for a women's clothing store. I was taught to guide the customer through the sale, not just point across the store and say, "The blouse you want is over there." I have taken those skills to heart when I collaborate with my own clients. Sometimes it's about making small talk and getting to know the person a little by asking how he or she is doing; other times, it's about finding ways that you're comfortable with to exceed a client's expectations.

As with just about everything else in the freelance world, there's no one way to do this, because it depends on your personality and the level of customer care you want to provide. The good thing is that you are the boss so you can set the tone for your business.

"The best tactic I've learned to develop a relationship with a client is to meet their needs and exceed their expectations," says Stephanie Jones (*www.cleverfinch.com*), a graphic designer and illustrator from Virginia.

One of her clients is a marketing director whose plate is always full. Jones meets with her regularly to explore projects coming down the pipeline so she's always first in line for them. "I help her put together time lines and lead times, and then I even put reminders on my calendar so I can follow up on these projects proactively," she says. "It's a win–win because it helps my overworked client stay on top of many projects...and it ensures that I'm the designer getting the work."

As a result, Jones says her client has come to think of her as a valued partner—not just a vendor. That's kept the working relationship positive and kept the projects flowing in. It's a good example of providing first-class customer service.

Friendly, Yet Professional

Christine Mason Miller (*www.christinemasonmiller.com*), an artist and author from California, says she bases her customer service approach based on *The Four Agreements* by Don Miguel Ruiz.

The first agreement is staying true to her word, so Miller follows through on what she promises. Second, she vows to do her best. When you give something your all, it's easier to feel at ease, say, if the client doesn't love your work at first glance. Third, Miller says not to make assumptions. This means giving people the benefit of the doubt and believing the best possible story until you have all the facts. Finally—and this is a tough one for many creatives—don't take criticism and feedback personally.

"I always tell potential clients to be honest with me about whatever work I am presenting to them. I literally do not take it personally," says Miller. "Rejection is part of this process. If I'm being rejected, it means I'm putting my work out there, and that is my job."

Miller says that nurturing a relationship doesn't always have to mean having an actual "relationship" at all—you can simply have a professional partnership. "I have found it is important to maintain a certain level of professionalism and, perhaps, emotional distance, instead of always trying to make the relationship be a friendship," she notes.

That's where many creatives struggle; they can't find a balance between being professional and infusing their own personality into the mix. As a solo-pro, you have a little more wiggle room but you still need to find that balance.

Simple Ways to Cultivate Client Relationships

One way I have developed relationships with clients is to share information I think they may find useful. It doesn't take much to send on an article that may appeal to a client. When I browse through requests from reporters for interviews in order to promote my business and my books, I often come across press opportunities for clients. Once, I read a listing from a reporter looking to speak with a construction contractor. I passed on the request to one of my customers, who wound up featured in a national publication. The client was elated that I thought of him, and the coverage was a boost for his business. In turn, I was happy that I could connect my client with the reporter, who turned to him for quotes in subsequent issues.

Even if you don't share information that winds up getting your client press coverage, it's a good idea to think of ways to connect that don't require much planning or effort on your part. Let these techniques help you foster relationships naturally, and over time. Remember that clients can spot a hungry contractor a mile away if you're not authentic with your intentions.

Take It From the Tackle Line: Do Your Job

Now you're thinking about cool ways to go above and beyond, but keep in mind one thing: The fact that so many solo-pros do not prioritize customer service means that, sometimes, just doing your job is beyond what a client expects. I hear from prospects that tell me the person they hired previously didn't complete a first draft on time or refused to revise the document with their feedback. They didn't even complete the job they were hired to do—let alone go that extra mile.

When everything is on the line for the New England Patriots, coach Bill Belichick tries to ground the players. Instead of getting them hyped up, he often tells them, "Do your job." What he means is that if everyone chips in doing what they are supposed to do, things will work out fine. I like to integrate that principle into my work. If I deliver a first draft and simply work with the client to incorporate any revisions, I will probably meet and exceed their expectations without doing much else, though I'll go above and beyond if given the opportunity, or when it makes sense to do so. Why? The freelance world is filled with dodgy contractors that don't deliver at all—never mind trying to forge client relationships.

It's not to say that you shouldn't go the extra mile for a client, but before you add all the extras make sure that you complete the job you were hired to do.

Angela Ferraro-Fanning (*www.1331design.com*), a graphic designer from New Jersey, says she always strives to be speedy when completing and submitting a round of revisions, letting her customers know the updates will not take more than two days. "This is something that's given me a competitive edge over other designers," she notes.

When her schedule allows, she works on revisions right away, though she admits some clients have taken her efforts for granted and expected an updated draft sooner than it was due. "I learned quickly that though my heart was in the right place, my prompt service was training clients to expect such and not giving me any wiggle room for meetings, meeting other deadlines, or even giving me time to think about the design solution," she notes.

So what's a freelancer to do? You want to exceed expectations but set boundaries at the same time. "Now, even if I have time to update the proof right away, I hold onto it for at least several hours. I go as far as to type up the e-mail, attach the proof, and then just save it in my draft e-mail folder for a while so it's there and ready for sending later on," Ferraro-Fanning explains.

I like how she rolls, because she's not working herself into a frenzy to please her clients, but she is still providing good customer service. Anything done before the deadline is a bonus, but just having it in when you say it will be done is enough to deliver straightforward service.

The "do your job" concept is quite applicable to your success as a freelancer. It's a good stepping stone, and you'd be surprised how many clients will rave about you simply for doing what you're supposed to!

Putting an End to Procrastination and Meeting Deadlines

When you take on a project, the client wants to know they can rely on you not only for good work, but good work *on time.* After all, their butts are on the line, too. When you provide that dependability, it leads to a good working relationship. Plus, it shows you respect their time.

If you turn in assignments late, I can almost guarantee that *if* the client retains you, they will stick you with last-minute requests and other personal boundary invasions. We teach others how we are willing to be treated.

I find two things are helpful when it comes to deadlines: set reasonable ones and alert yourself to them. This sounds simple, but again, you'd be surprised how many solo-pros not only deliver subpar work but turn it in late, if at all. Set deadlines you can work with so you don't wind up having to ask for an extension; that's a "get out of jail free" card that you *only* want to use if you absolutely have to.

Other clients may not set a deadline at all, which can sound like a free pass in the beginning. If you wind up procrastinating on a job that's due "sometime in the next month," you may not be able to accept last-minute projects that come in—often with lucrative rush fees. I like to work ahead of time on projects so I have the option of taking others that come in. My availability is one of my competitive advantages; my clients know I am most likely to accommodate projects because I manage my time well.

Rising Above Creative Differences

Another aspect of client relations involves how you interact with clients if things feel tense. Thus far, we talked about ways to form client relations; now we'll delve into how you can maintain and improve them despite common obstacles.

Regardless of how polite you are or the fact that all of your clients may be your favorites, when your services or products do not align with what the customer expects, it can take a toll on the relationship. How you deal with creative differences is what distinguishes you from other solo-pros. You can't please everyone, but if you know how to resolve issues, you can "win back" the client and get a glowing review.

I have had discrepancies with clients that, largely because of the way I handled things, still got me additional projects and referrals. A creative disagreement does not have to spell disaster for your relationship with a client; in fact, it's really part of the creative process.

It is normal for creative differences to occur. The artistic field is subjective, so it's inevitable that the client may not adore your first take on something. That's why building revisions into your fee is advisable. Then you can show the client that you are committed to assisting them in making the product just right.

Graphic designer Ferraro-Fanning recalls landing a job with a client that wanted all new marketing collateral. She was replacing a designer who had assisted the company to establish its identity, but that relationship ended because arguments ensued over design ideas. Ferraro-Fanning got to work on the well-paying project by compiling an estimate and originating some fresh designs. But the client wasn't really interested in her concepts.

"They really didn't want my suggestions nor did they take me very seriously; they drew up their own mock-ups with pen and paper and would scan them in and send them to me via e-mail," says Ferraro-Fanning. She says it was not long before it was clear to her that they did not want a partner. "They wanted a software puppet," claims Ferraro-Fanning.

She continued working on the project, but couldn't seem to shake her feelings that the designs were not representative of her best work.

After a few months, she ended the relationship with the client. To this day, Ferraro-Fanning says she wonders if she had taken a professional approach by upholding her standards—or if she let her own ego get in the way. It's a tough call, because as freelancers we want to keep our clients satisfied. Yet it's hard to put your name—or your time—into work that is what I like to call "sucktastic."

Perhaps in this case, she should have finished the project and kept the final materials far, far away from your portfolio. Otherwise, like Ferraro-Fanning, you're left wondering if you did the right thing.

I have had the same thing happen with clients that have transformed my first draft into something subpar. In that case, I only make sure there are no glaring errors and let them go on their way. The client has hired you for your expertise, but you need to incorporate their feedback, too, even if you think it is not necessary. If you find yourself arguing with clients to defend your work more often than not, you may be acting too forceful with your talent, and that could push clients away—fast! The client may not always be "right," but they have hired you to do a job, and they are entitled to have input in the final deliverable.

Some creatives may not have to deal with revisions or feedback. In that case, consider yourself lucky. When you are commissioned to complete a project, however, be prepared to accept some input from time to time. Sure, it sucks to feel like your work isn't good enough, but that's not the case most of the time. Creative materials are very subjective, and it's all right for someone else to have a different opinion.

What situations have you encountered in your business that you feel you didn't handle correctly?

"Early on, a design partner threatened me with a small claims court suit when the end client canceled the project in the 11th hour. I panicked and sent a rather unpleasant e-mail to the client. Fortunately, my sales coach talked me through the situation, and I fell on my sword, calling the client and apologizing profusely. We sorted things out, worked out the payment, and became good friends in the end. I should have sought the guidance before making an ass of myself."

—Mistina Picciano, president, *www.marketitwrite.com*

Working With Mean Girls, Menaces, and Jerks

Taking feedback from a client is one thing—but when they act mean or disrespectful, or get downright nasty, things can move quickly to a whole new level. You may be working with a client who is aloof or rude and figure that your customer service responsibilities are moot—no way! Even a "meanie" can warm up in some instances. Some of my clients have not been exactly a breeze to work with, but I strived to do my best and work with them. As a result, I got more work or a nice recommendation. In some cases, that testimonial paid off because others knew what a "tough act" the client was!

Like most of you, I have had my fair share of clients that I didn't want to work with. Those who know me understand that just because I may not like a person does not mean I will turn a project away. If the pay is good or the exposure is going to benefit me, I will likely work with a prospect that I am not particularly fond of.

I can think of one client who retained me a few times that has been particularly a challenge to remain kind to. My close friends often tell me, "Oh, just dump the client; you're *self-employed*!" You and I know it's not always that easy, particularly if you want to *stay* self-employed.

I've learned to work with this client and not take anything they say personally. I choose my battles, and try to focus on the paychecks rather than the drama that sometimes ensues. I found that once I shifted my perspective to appreciate the positives and stand up for what I need, the relationship flowed much better.

If, on the other hand, you find that a client becomes more of a "drive-by" target, you may want to rethink sustaining the relationship. There are only so many things you can do to make things work. When a client gets blatantly mean and rude, I tend to wrap up the project and part ways. If they're just hyper-critical but know how to stay nice for the most part, I'm willing to work with a less-than-desirable personality. As a solo-pro, you have to find a balance and determine what you will put up with—and what you won't. Just don't be too picky or you won't stay in business for long.

What areas of your personality can damage a client relationship?

"The main tool I use to keep my negative tendencies in check is to wait at least 24 hours before sending an e-mail in a charged situation—to do nothing, sit still, and give the situation some breathing room."

—Christine Mason Miller, artist/writer,
www.christinemasonmiller.com

Sweet success
Going the Extra Mile—or Miles
Graphic designer Angela Ferraro-Fanning (*www.1331design.com*) from New Jersey was hired to design a logo, brochures, and a Web site for a client. The necessary programming for the Web site sign-up function was beyond Ferraro-Fanning's know-how, so she retained a freelance programmer to assist.

After experiencing communications issues with the programmer, Ferraro-Fanning's client called on a Saturday to let her know she was fed up. Though working weekends is a no-no for Ferraro-Fanning, she could sense the matter was urgent and met with the client that day to discuss the problem. "I needed to take the situation into my own hands before I got fired for the programmer's poor performance," she recalls. "I decided rather than blame-shift frustrations on the programmer, I would make it clear to the client that I empathized with her. I wanted her to know that I was on her side, not the programmer's, and that her happiness and project were my priorities."

Ferraro-Fanning told the client if she wanted to fire the programmer, she would do it that weekend so they could move forward. The programmer got the boot, and the ladies found a programming solution.

"I think [she] was impressed I drove over to her studio on a weekend to talk with her so quickly," Ferraro-Fanning says. Ferraro-Fanning says that she felt closer to her client because, in hearing her out, it created a mutual respect and camaraderie.

Beginner Mishap
How Soon Is Too Soon?

When Brian Casel (*www.casjam.com*), a Web site designer and developer in Connecticut, started freelancing, he wanted to excel at delivering for clients. One mistake he says he made repeatedly was responding too quickly to client requests.

"It can actually backfire on you," says Casel, who used to respond to e-mails within minutes and answered the phone each time it rang regardless of what time of day it was. At first, clients perked up to his snappy service, but Casel soon found out that they wanted that immediate response all the time. "When I was finally able to take my first vacation, my clients freaked out when I wasn't available to answer an e-mail that came in on a Sunday," he notes.

Eventually, Casel decided to enact a strict phone policy: He almost never answers unexpected phone calls now. Calls must be scheduled at least a day in advance. And as for that pesky, overflowing e-mail in-box, Casel says he tries to check it twice per day or dedicate time in the morning to respond to requests. He no longer takes phone calls or reads work e-mail on weekends and vacations, either.

The results have been beneficial for his peace of mind, and it enables him to provide better client service as well. "Clients appreciate my consistency and I keep my sanity. My project work benefits from the added focus as well," Casel adds.

Chapter 8

Setting Boundaries

In delivering top-notch customer service, you may find that it tests your boundaries. You may go the extra mile for a client, but that same client can also wind up trying to take more than you want to give. This is why having boundaries in place is so critical. The right boundaries can prevent you from being treated poorly, and form a foundation to make sure you work efficiently and earn an optimal amount of money.

Certain boundaries may be unspoken rules; in fact, you probably do not want to bring up every possible stipulation you have when you are prospecting. Just because some of your boundaries may not be in writing doesn't mean they are any less important. What are you willing to deal with—and what are the deal-breakers for you as an individual? You probably expect others to act pleasantly, but some people don't. What will you do if you encounter a meanie?

Let's say you are working on a project and included two rounds of revisions. After you go back and forth with the client twice, the project looks good. Then the client wants to make "just a few more" changes. That client seems fairly happy with your work so far, sent your deposit on time, and has been nice, so you don't see the harm in spending another half hour on a third round of revisions.

What if the revisions take you an hour, and after you submit them to the client, they wants "just a few more?" You've already gone beyond the scope of what was outlined in your contract. What can you do? How do you know that if you give more, the client won't want a fifth round of revisions? How do you cope with the feeling that you are being taken advantage of?

Exhausting yourself in this kind of loop doesn't mean you deliver exceptional customer service—it means you are letting clients walk all over you!

Establishing boundaries is imperative. I'm not saying be super stingy about offering a third round of revisions if your contract only included two—but if you keep giving your time away, you are making less money, are diverting your attention away from other possibilities, and may eventually feel like a perpetual doormat.

You can spell out certain boundaries (you can dictate how many revisions you will complete before having to bill for additional rounds hourly), but others aren't so easy to articulate. I do not tell clients, "You better be on time for our conference call or else," because one would assume being punctual is a given. Even though I have been stood up for phone meetings, I usually give a client a second chance to make it on time. I would definitely rethink the partnership after two missed calls, however, especially when I carve out time in my schedule to be there.

When it comes to your rules and your procedures—that general "how I work" babble—you have to give the client some idea of what they are in for. Specify how and when customers can reach you. Let them know about your editing policy. There are other boundaries that you have to put up as you go because unexpected situations arise.

For example, I worked with a client recently that promised they would gather facts from their client so I could incorporate the details into my copy. When I turned in the first draft, they seemed shocked that details were missing. In response, I politely noted that I hadn't received information from them that they had agreed to give me. I wasn't about to spend more time conducting research on information they said they had; it would have taken a few extra hours and my rate would go down. I let the client know politely that I would be happy to add more but would tack on my hourly rate or expand the quote if a request exceeded the scope of work we agreed upon. In being up front, I set the expectations, so if more work is needed, the client knows they will pay additional money for it.

In this situation, I think it paid off because after reviewing my comments, the client was quick to let me know they were sorry they did not include that information in the original scope of work, would pay extra for me to do the research they never did, and they would make sure they had research ready or would inform me if it needed to be done for future projects. It may seem like a small detail, but essentially, I told that client they could not leave out information and then expect me to fill in the gaps as if it were my mistake.

This is what good boundaries do: They protect you and prevent you from doormat-ville.

Do you see why setting boundaries is so important? Whether it is something you have to say to a client from the start of a project, or the way you stick up for yourself if you hit a bump in the road, you will be much happier in the long run if you are clear about what you will and will not accept. I'm not saying fight every possible fight, but do it when you think the situation may happen again, or has in the past. Convey your message clearly and constructively, simply letting the client know what you need going forward.

Your Business, Your Rules?

Boundaries are fantastic, but you don't want to go rule-happy on your clients—especially hitting them with a ton of rules on possible scenarios that may not apply to them. I have found that giving prospective clients an idea of how you work is a good plan. That way, you set the expectations. This is one way to set limits; we'll talk about how to stick to your guns in just a bit.

For instance, I outline information on my Web site about how I do business from explaining how I handle consultations and payments to the way I account for editing time. I have an entire page devoted to helping a client understand "what happens next."

Soon after Sara Robbins-Page launched her jewelry design company, Heavens to Bessie (*www.heavenstobessie.com*), on a full-time basis, the Maryland-based artisan was approached by a boutique owner who wanted to carry her distinctive line of handcrafted jewelry. "I had never done a wholesale order before but the opportunity for an order of that size and the exposure that the sale would give was simply too good to pass up," recalls Robbins-Page. Because she had just taken her side business full-time and had never sold her jewelry wholesale, she didn't have the policies in place for large-scale orders. "I went ahead with the order anyway, sending it off with a simple invoice," Robbins-Page explains.

As a result of not having a more detailed process and rules in place, it took about seven months to receive a payment. Robbins-Page said she should have communicated those policies to the buyer. "Had I done this, I would have saved myself from a lot of stress and frustration," she admits.

What's the best way to make sure I don't get stiffed by a client?

"Of course, every situation is different. I always require a deposit upfront, usually 50 percent of the total project fee, and it is clearly stated in my contract that this is non-refundable. So no matter what happens down the line, my time and work is at least partially paid for no matter what. After working with many clients over the course of your first few years, you'll get much better at spotting the red flags of potential nightmare clients."

—Brian Casel, Web site designer/developer, *www.casjam.com*

What to Base Your Boundaries On

Having a few guidelines in place lays the groundwork to establish, and then enforce, your boundaries. Think about some of these components when you develop your business practices.

→ **Scope of work.** What, exactly, will a project entail? It may not just be writing, as it is in my case. Often you have to collect information via phone calls and strategize with a team. Ask about these secondary tasks to build time into your quote.

→ **Consultations.** Will your consultation be over the phone or e-mail? Is it free? During what hours will you accept calls? How much information should a client have handy before they call? What if they need a follow-up consult? Will you charge for that?

When a client calls initially, I don't really consider that a consult. I'm available via the phone during most business days to respond to quick inquiries. When the client decides they want to use my services and I have a signed contract and deposit in hand, that's when I want to collect more detailed information on the project via a free consultation. They get *one* unless they think they will need more, which I build into my price. I state that one consultation is complimentary; for the rest I charge by the hour.

I had a client call me today that wanted me to drive more than an hour away to *discuss* ideas for his project. I had to let him know that I do not travel on-site to work unless the client has retained me for a project. Boundary—check!

→ **Editing/revision process.** I let the client know that editing is a normal part of the process and I am here to shepherd them through the development of their content. Sometimes I note that it is possible they will not fall in love with the first draft and it is okay if that happens; I will work with them to get it just right, and they can use the revisions included as a satisfaction guarantee, so to say. Communicating this off the bat has saved me from dealing with overly critical clients that expect complete perfection from the start. Writing is too subjective for most first drafts to be "perfect," anyway.

→ **The contract.** Let clients know when you first communicate that you require a signed contract. This will scare off clients that are slow to pay or are not professional, and let viable clients know you mean business. I used to feel timid in bringing up my contract and would mention it after the consultation, but then I felt like I was dropping a bomb on the client. Now I let clients know on my Web site and when we converse initially that I require a signed written agreement prior to starting work. I turn it into a selling point because the contract ensures they receive what I have promised, too.

→ **Time line.** Even clients that do not require a "rush" seem to want things yesterday. I inform clients that most projects can be turned around within a week, and to contact me to set up a time line. I am also careful to tell them that I do not start on the project until I receive a signed contract and 50-percent deposit. So if it is Monday and I say can get a first draft to them on the following Monday, they need to get that contract and deposit in that day. If I do not receive the deposit and contract until Friday afternoon, they are *not* getting the first draft Monday. Be clear about your time line, accounting for administrative time, too. Sometimes it takes a few days to receive a signed contract and deposit, so anticipate it into your time line.

→ **Deposit.** If you want half of the fee upfront, tell your clients about this from the start. Also, let them know when the balance is due. You may want to bring up that balances are due for completed work, as some weasels will try to insist they shouldn't have to pay if they are not satisfied.

→ **Pricing.** Every project is different, and you do not always know what variables will come into play until you speak to someone. Wait until after that call to either call back or e-mail with your quote. I collect some details about a project before throwing out a quote or proposal. I never quote directly over the phone because I don't want to be roped into that price should I find that project will take longer and have to raise my fee.

→ **Payment.** It is only fair to let a potential or existing client know what types of payment you accept. For me, it is strictly check and PayPal. Whatever type of payment you take, make sure to specify it. If you charge a deposit, make sure to stipulate when the balance of your payment is due.

→ **Communication.** Specify if you will include information-gathering meetings or calls. Let a client know if you will be reachable by phone or e-mail. Some freelancers give clients unlimited phone support; I prefer to set up a call if need be and let clients know that additional "face time" will cost them. Most respect my honesty because I state it from the start.

Must-Read
The Art of Extreme Self-Care: Transforming Your Life One Step at a Time **by Cheryl Richardson**

Putting It out There

You would think, for example, that a client knows not to call you five times a day or e-mail you on weekends, but that's not the case. That's why setting your rules—and then conveying your practices—is vital.

When a client knows that you don't take business calls after, say, 5 p.m., they probably are not likely to call. If they do and you do not answer, you don't have to feel bad because it states your business hours on your Web site or in your contract. Although you probably should not spell out how many times a day a client can e-mail or call you, it is important to tell them what the typical process involves so they have an idea of what they can—and can't—get away with. There are three ways to educate clients about your processes:

1. On your Web site or over e-mail.
2. On the phone.
3. In your contract.

Although the contract is a good place to put a note about revisions or a reference about posting the client's work in your portfolio, you can't really cover the full scope of your process in the contract. The rest of the details are better left for your Web site or a phone call, or as issues come up.

Enforcement, Plain and Simple

We've talked about the kinds of boundaries you may want to put in place. Now let's explore how you should enforce them when you feel a client or colleague getting too close for comfort.

Jay Rogers (*www.jayrodesign.com*), a Georgia-based designer and illustrator, said he had issues as a beginner because clients always seemed to want more than what they hired him to do.

Rogers recalls a client who wanted to make some complex revisions to backgrounds they previously had approved. "Since the request was beyond the number of revisions they had already received, I was able to point back to that statement of the scope of work and negotiate a fee for that additional work," Rogers says. "I couldn't have had that leverage otherwise, so it was invaluable!"

Now, he writes out a clear, detailed scope of work that includes the number of revisions, specifics on the deliverables, and other details. Not only does specifying the scope of work upfront help your client relationships; Rogers says it can "save your butt...and your bottom line."

How can I avoid scope creep other than specifying what the project entails—and doesn't—in my contract?

"Include up to three rounds of revisions in your contract and then specify an hourly rate for any revisions or additions beyond that point. When presenting a revised design to a client, label your e-mail and the submitted design document to indicate which round of revisions they are on. This helps set client expectations and eliminate surprises. Many clients will stop tinkering with a design once they realize it will be an additional fee. That being said, don't overlook the opportunity to 'super-size' your project by selling additional services and features."

—Amber Timmerman, graphic designer/Web designer,
www.mintyfreshdesign.com

Susan Johnston (*www.susan-johnston.com*), a freelance writer from Massachusetts, remembers working with a client that assumed taglines were included in her Web site content. The client never mentioned taglines, and Johnston thought she had clearly outlined what was included in the project. What should she have done: give a little or resist completely?

"I knew it wouldn't take too long to brainstorm some taglines so I sent her a few ideas as a value-add to keep her happy," says Johnston. The client did not like her concepts, however, and asked her to send more. "I'd already given her more than agreed upon, so I felt I needed to put my foot down," she says. Johnston told the client she would be happy to create more tagline suggestions, but because it was not part of the original project scope, she would revisit the fee. "She got the message and chose one of the original taglines I originally sent," Johnston adds.

I like the way Johnston handled it. She knew that penning a few extra phrases wouldn't take her a lot of time, and used her judgment when going the extra mile—as well as when she should hold her ground. When the client didn't like what she had come up with, she reminded the client who she had already gone out of the scope of work, and that additional time would cost more.

Aubre Andrus (*www.aubreandrus.com*), a freelance writer from Seattle, encountered scope creep when one of her favorite blogs hired her to write content. After, she found out they only paid $50 for a post, which entailed writing, shooting and editing photos, coding the post into WordPress, and participating in weekly conference calls. "I didn't even finish one assignment before realizing that although this client would look amazing in my portfolio, it wasn't worth my time," recalls Andrus.

Andrus says she has learned her lesson about taking jobs where she does not receive all the details on how much work is really involved from the get-go. Again, these situations are not necessarily the client's fault; as solo-pros, we have to ask the right questions to determine the full latitude of the work before we lay blame on the client for scope creeping.

I think many freelancers do not consider that these scenarios could play out when they start, but most seasoned pros are all too familiar with them. It is, as are many aspects of being self-employed, something that you learn to deal with as you go—and something that definitely needs to be expressed to the client the moment an issue arises. In telling customers about your processes from the start, you can generally nip these sorts of things in the bud and move on to a satisfying relationship.

Protect Your Time

I am a self-proclaimed workaholic, but I have certainly learned to set and respect my own schedule as the years have gone on. I only work on weekends when I really need or want to. Otherwise, I have to remind myself to shut down on Friday afternoons.

In recent years, I've stopped answering the phone after 5 p.m. and even noted business hours on my Web site. I am not the only creative professional that has had to establish boundaries when it comes to my time. Stephanie Jones (*www.cleverfinch.com*), a graphic designer and illustrator from Virginia, is a new mom juggling work and parenting.

Soon after she became a mother, one of her clients continued to call her several times a day despite her reminders that she is not available by the phone for most of the day. She has directed the client to leave a voice mail or send an e-mail in order to keep projects moving forward. "I still struggle with this and at this time have included 'Client Hours: 10 a.m.–2 p.m.' on my e-mail signature so clients are aware that I am not available to them from 9 a.m. to 5 p.m. This way, I don't feel guilty when I can't pick up a call," she says.

Must-Read
My So-Called Freelance Life: How to Survive and Thrive as a Creative Professional for Hire by **Michelle Goodman**

Adios, It's Over: The Break-Up

It's no wonder that many of us equate client relationships to dating. You're either happily in love, nearing a bitter break-up, or dealing with a "spark" that is readily dwindling, yet hanging on anyway. There's nothing wrong if each client relationship does not give you butterflies; sometimes you may not love the project or the client but the pay is good, or vice versa. Or you may be hanging on to a client for another reason; maybe the brand recognition they provide is a benefit. That's okay.

There will be clients that are not worth sticking it out for. Maybe you're not interested anymore, the client has gone too far, they are becoming increasingly difficult or rude—or heck, they could even be "cheating" on you by using a competitor!

For whatever reason you find to sever ties, splitting from a client can be difficult because you probably don't mean the client any ill will. Sometimes, working together just isn't a good fit. Luckily, the rules of business are a little more lenient than in dating. For instance, some solo-pros find it more acceptable to let a client know you no longer wish to work together over e-mail; it's a little more acceptable than dumping a boyfriend or girlfriend that way, right? You may prefer to confront a client on the phone or in person. Depending on how you word the communication, it doesn't have to turn into a fight. After wrapping up a project, it's not unheard of for solo-pros to simply stop communicating with a client as a signal that they no longer wish to work together.

I rarely have to "dump" clients I don't want to work with anymore because they either only need one-time copywriting assistance or I refer them to another writer. I have told a few clients that I didn't think I was a good fit for their projects; that's a widely accepted "thanks but no thanks" way to word things without having to go into specifics. Sometimes you really are *not* the best fit for a gig.

Jones knows what it's like to realize it is time to part ways with a client. She has ended two client relationships during her career. "My clients, in both cases, revealed themselves over time to be unprofessional and poor planners. They were both uninterested in paying attention to details...and not surprisingly they would exceed scope and become combative when I would let them know in advance there would be an additional charge if they needed the extra work done," she recalls.

If you terminate a relationship, try not to think of it as failure. Maybe your client has acted like a butthead, or maybe you want to set your sights on something new. That's all right.

"The great part about these experiences is that although they stunk, I will likely never have a client like that again because I can spot the warning signs a mile away. Learning the hard way is tough, but you often learn the lesson quickly and are not doomed to repeat the same mistake over and over again," Jones says.

Boundaries are essential not only to keep your sanity, but to remain productive. These processes you devise and policies you establish may not necessarily go into your contract, but that doesn't mean they don't matter or deserve respect.

That's why it is critical you discuss these things with your client ahead of time and respond to matters, firmly, if they transpire. Set the tone from the get-go—then the creativity can commence!

Sweet Success
It's All in the Details

After Susan Johnston (*www.susan-johnston.com*), a Massachusetts-based freelance writer, reviewed a client's Web site copy needs, she put together a quote based on research time, a phone call, and one round of revisions if needed.

Because she works remotely with practically all of her clients, Johnston never asked if an in-person meeting was necessary. The client, though, was expecting some face-time. "Of course, I didn't ask and she didn't mention it until after she'd paid a deposit and I was starting," she said. "I knew that meeting with her would take several hours including travel time and I hadn't included this in the project quote...I told her I'd be happy to meet with her, but we'd have to adjust the fee since it was outside the original scope of the project."

After that, the client decided a phone conversation would work just as well. The project went smoothly from there, but is a constant reminder that you have to cover all bases when putting together a quote—and stick to your guns if the project expands beyond its original scope.

Beginner Mishap
More Than a Public Relations Nightmare

Seattle based writer Michelle Goodman (*www.anti9to5guide.com*) remembers a time as a rookie when she agreed to publicize a dance show for a husband-and-wife team. She and the clients agreed verbally that she would put in 40 hours to promote the show, which would include drafting a press release and trying to secure coverage from media outlets. In true novice fashion, she did not collect a deposit upfront and agreed to collect payment at the end of the assignment.

The client asked her to attend performances and meetings, something she didn't consider when putting together her estimate. Some of the requests were a little far-fetched, she jokes, but she admits she was at fault for not setting boundaries from the start.

After putting in at least 80 hours, not only did her rate go down by half; she never got paid. Without a contract in place, what did she have to leverage? "Having a contract or e-mail agreement would have helped," she admits. "I was young and impressionable and I had no boundaries, I just agreed to everything." Goodman says it was annoying to realize she had been taken advantage of, especially because she could have prevented it. Nowadays, Goodman never starts a project without a contract and a deposit in hand.

Chapter 9

The Well-Rounded Freelancer

Although a strong business requires you to be business-savvy, a huge part of your career does, indeed, revolve around your artistic gifts. Advance your skills and you can boost your creative edge along with your value as a competitor in the industry. You don't have to earn a degree in your field to excel. Other options include obtaining certificates, taking courses, joining industry organizations, networking, and becoming a thought leader in your field. Let's take a look at the many paths you can take to enhance your skillset and stand out from other solo-pros.

Taking Your Education to the Next Level

Taking courses can be useful to enhance your professional know-how and form connections. Susan Johnston (*www.susan-johnston.com*), a freelance writer from Massachusetts, earned her Bachelor of Science in Communications from Boston University in 2005, and obtained a Certificate in Writing for Professional Communication from Emerson College in 2010. (Many colleges today offer certificates to allow those with a bachelor's degree to specialize in a field without earning as many credits as would be necessary for a master's degree.)

"It was...less of a time commitment than an MFA but still gave me something tangible that I wouldn't get from a...one-off class," she says. Overall, Johnston says the certificate program gave her feedback and polished her communications acumen. "I don't think it's convinced clients to hire me per se, but it certainly helped hone my skills and connected me with a wonderful network of professionals," she says. "Oftentimes prospects see Emerson College on my resume and tell me they're also alums, which creates an instant commonality and easy talking point."

Johnston says if freelancers are satisfied with the level of work they produce and are landing the clients they want, they do not necessarily need to enter a program; sometimes a single class can be just as valuable to learn something new or reinvigorate your creativity.

Why should freelancers continue their education to improve their talent?

"Most freelancers went to school to study a specific craft: design, writing, photography, etc. We didn't take business classes because they weren't required. When we were in school, we didn't see a need to take them, thinking we'd graduate and be working for an agency or company. Whether by chance or by choice, once out freelancing, we need to know how to run a business. That's why continuing education is so important, especially if you want to move to the top tier of freelancers and conduct business more professionally."

—Julie Cortés, co-founder, *www.freelancersu.com*

Resource
A few sites with useful courses include www.howdesignuniversity. com, www.teamtreehouse.com, www.codecademy.com, www.iwanet. org, www.bediabistro.com, and www.poynter.com. Fine artists can typically find courses locally because the arts tend to be more hands-on.

Learning About Business Basics

Discovering how to operate a business can be just as beneficial as taking a course on a new software application or crafting technique.

Luckily, a few fellow solo-pros have gained notoriety for aiding freelancers in success. Ed Gandia, who runs the International Freelancers Academy (*www.internationalfreelancersacademy.com*), is one of them. Julie Cortés is another that's putting useful information out there to arm freelancers for success.

Cortés, a Kansas-based copywriter, started Freelancers University (*www.freelancersu.com*) in 2011 as a continuing education portal for freelancers. Freelancers University once offered a course titled "How to Grow a Pair and Train Your Clients." As part of the class, she covered topics such as setting and sticking to business hours, informing clients on scheduling and communications, and using industry standards such as contracts, deposits, and payments.

"A soft-spoken, divorced, single mother in her early 50s attended the class, primarily to learn how to deal with a client she was struggling with," Cortés explains. "By the end of the class, you could tell she was completely empowered to go train her client who was taking advantage of her and her schedule." The next time Cortés saw the woman, she was elated. The class had given her the advice necessary to put her foot down and stop letting the client take advantage of her schedule. "That was just music to my ears," says Cortés. "I've always had a love for freelancers' rights...probably because I experienced way too many injustices when I first started out in my freelance copywriting career."

What do you find is the biggest area freelancers need to know more about?

"I think it's important for freelancers to understand our industry standards (such as having a contract). So many businesses—large and small, agency and corporate alike—have this mindset that they can dictate how freelancers run their businesses. This is so not true! There are plenty of industry standards for solo creative professionals that, if we all just knew what they were—and practiced them, we could start turning the tables on these businesses who like to think they can take advantage of the solopreneur."

—Julie Cortés, co-founder, *www.freelancersu.com*

Certifications

In discussing Johnston's certificate, it's important to note that hers was an academic credential; certifications from industry organizations can be just as valuable. Trade groups administer these certifications.

My resume-writing certification, for example, is backed by a prominent career coaching and resume organization. It looks fantastic on my resume and in my biography, and has led to many gigs and provided several networking opportunities.

Certifications are not a must, but they do lend an air of credibility to your brand. For example, if you build Web sites you may want to or earn a certificate in Web site development. Some groups will require you to maintain membership to hold your certification. Poke around on-line at forums specific to your industry and ask other creatives about any applicable credentials that may benefit you.

Joining the Club: Industry Organizations

You don't have to enter a classroom to expand your abilities. Trade organizations exist for just about every profession out there, and can be a respected resource to learn more *and* expand your network at the same time.

Johnston is a member of the American Society for Journalists and Authors (ASJA) and has been to a few conferences—even speaking at two of them. The ASJA offers a Grievance Committee that can advise her on financial issues and assist her in obtaining payment. She also joined *www.freelancesuccess.com,* a paid on-line community that enables her to share leads, find writing markets, and compare notes on pay rates with other solo-pros.

Jay Rogers (*www.jayrodesign.com*), a Georgia-based designer and illustrator, says joining his local AIGA (formerly the American Institute of Graphic Arts) chapter has been instrumental to his career. He leads an ongoing roundtable event for studio owners and freelancers. Not only does he get solutions from others, but it gives him a sounding board to commiserate when he needs to vent. "It has been invaluable to me to meet others in the same position as me," he says.

Lisa L. Owens (*www.llowens.com*), a writer and editor from Seattle, is a long-time member of both the Editorial Freelancers Association

(EFA) and the Society of Children's Book Writers and Illustrators (SCBWI). She says she always recommends that rookie freelancers get involved when they join a group. "You are always free to just pay your membership fee and wait for the benefits to roll in...but when was the last time you experienced a boon to any aspect of your work life from doing nothing?" she says.

Owens continues to volunteer with the EFA because she says it has helped her form other professional connections that she will benefit from for the rest of her career. She organizes chapter events and monitors the organization's Facebook page; two activities she says have helped her meet colleagues while staying current on industry news. "Self-employed creatives so often work in relative isolation," she notes. "The right professional organization provides you with a receptive group of coworkers that reminds you that you're not alone."

The nice thing about industry organizations is that they can offer interesting seminars, access to health insurance, and other benefits along with exclusive content and on-line forums. These groups can also be fantastic for staying on top of your industry and connecting with others in your field.

Why should freelancers consider joining a professional association?

"Assuming the group is a good fit with your professional niche, the membership fee usually comes back to you in the form of paid-work opportunities. Potential clients might see your information in the member directory; you might meet new clients at association events or get referrals from other members. A prospect might see the group listed on your LinkedIn profile and take you more seriously."

—Lisa L. Owens, writer/editor, *www.llowens.com*

Networking for Professional Development

We discussed networking as a way to market yourself and generate leads, but the professional development side of networking can be just as useful.

Networking for professional development involves connecting with colleagues for support rather than leads. Typically you would join a group of professionals in your field; in my case, I could join a writers' group to discuss my work, gain feedback, and receive support. You do not have to spend tons of money or even venture out of the house to do this; several on-line forums along with social media can link you with colleagues.

Some organizations may not offer seminars with formal learning, but that doesn't mean you can't learn a lot. Explore the group first; see if you can go to a meeting to check it out or chat up some of the members on-line. They may offer educational speakers and useful seminars. If for nothing else, you will definitely meet some cool people with the same unique vibe you have!

Branching Out for Lasting Success

A good way to expand your horizons as a creative professional has nothing to do with education. In diversifying your brand, you can offer *related services* and set up *alternative sources of income.* For example, I am not only a copywriter; I write magazine articles and books, too. Those related services integrate my skills, and are also personal passions I have leveraged to make extra income.

I know many Web site designers that have taken on Web development as a means to offer complementary services so their clients can use them to create a logo *and* a Web presence. Some Web developers possess copywriting capabilities too, so they can offer complete Web site services to offer design *and* copy.

As you become more well-versed in your business, you may want to consider how to spread your wings. It's not only a good way to bring in extra income; it ensures that you don't get "bored" doing the same thing all the time. Let your brand evolve and consider branching out with what you have to offer. You probably know how to do that once you put your mind to it. After all, if you are a painter, you can probably segue very easily into becoming a watercolor teacher. This uses your skills so you can offer related services and earn money from them, too.

Alternative Revenue Stream # I: Become a Speaker

California-based Luke Mysse (*www.lukemysse.com*) likes to call himself an "activator" more than a graphic or Web designer because he stimulates marketing platforms through design. Mysse has a passion for sharing his message, which is why it was a natural move to add speaking to his professional repertoire. "Speaking was one of those things that I felt like I should be doing," says Mysse.

After giving a talk at a local AIGA event, he got a call to speak at the HOW Creative Freelancer Conference. Since then, he's spoken for several business audiences at conferences and other events—he loves it. Mysse believes that you have to have some sort of speaking talent to begin, and advises novice speakers to join Toastmasters International (or similar groups that focus on professional skills) to reinforce your abilities.

The secret to his success is authenticity. Mysse ties his own struggles as a freelancer into his talks and lets himself become a bit vulnerable during the speeches. That's helped him to connect to audience members, which is what he believes keeps speaking gigs coming in.

How do you know if speaking is right for you? So long as you have a relevant message and can elevate it to a level where you are comfortable delivering a presentation, speaking can be fulfilling—and a boundless source of extra income.

What makes a good speaking presentation?

"I think the honesty and transparency thing is big. I think being who you are and not trying to be something else is huge. People connect with people who are real."

—Luke Mysse, designer/speaker, *www.lukemysse.com*

Alternative Revenue Stream #2: Write a Book

Another way to advance your career is to publish your own book. Let me illustrate the different publishing models, because I've used different strategies for each of the books I have published.

When you start out with a book idea, you probably want to "go big or go home" and land a huge publisher. You want your book in all the stores; who doesn't? The reality is that it can be hard to publish a book, particularly non-fiction, because landing a big publisher is largely based on your platform; your ability to write can sometimes come secondary. To get to the big guys, you generally have to have an agent;

some won't even look at your idea without an agent to shepherd the deal. An agent is also a good "in" when approaching medium-sized and smaller publishers. Acquiring an agent is challenging; you do not hire the agent, the agent has to agree to represent you (typically based on a proposal), then he or she sells your work to a publisher.

You can also approach certain publishers on your own; in general, smaller or niche publishers are open to unagented submissions.

Thanks to self-publishing, anyone can publish a book via either a self-publishing service, or simply offering your book on-line. If you self-publish with a service such as iUniverse, you can create a physical book to sell. Many freelancers also create short e-books and publish them on their Web sites.

Must-Reads

The Well-Fed Writer: Financial Self-Sufficiency as a Commercial Freelancer in Six Months or Less by Peter Bowerman and *The Renegade Writer: A Totally Unconventional Guide to Freelance Writing Success* by Diana Burrell and Linda Formichelli

Jim Krause (*www.jimkrausedesign.com*) never intended to be a writer. The designer, illustrator, and photographer from Washington says he had come up with a brainstorming technique that he thought may be helpful for others. That's when he derived the idea behind his book, *Idea Index.* He took a different foray into the publishing world: He skipped the idea of landing a literary agent and chose not to self-publish. Instead, he came up with a book proposal, then went to a bookstore, and wrote down the names of publishers who were putting out the best books on similar topics. One ignored him, another passed on the idea, and the final (HOW Books) wound up publishing the book.

As a result, Krause has penned more than a dozen books covering the creative field. He says that the exposure from being published can be significant; plus, it can help you secure more clients and, ultimately, better rates.

"From my perspective and experience, there is no definite right or wrong way to get something published," he says. "The main thing is simply to do *something.* If that something works, fine. If not, try it some more or try something else."

Resource

www.writersmarket.com **publishes** *Writer's Market* **yearly, a book and on-line database packed with listings of publishers and agents. Also visit** *www.pred-ed.com, www.sfwa.org/for-authors/writer-beware, and www.absolutewrite.com* **to learn about publishing.**

Alternative Revenue Stream #3: Try Your Hand...er, Keyboard...at Blogging

You don't have to pen a book to be a valuable contributor in the creative world. Blogging has opened up doors for plenty of freelancers looking to share their insights and connect with others.

All you need is a Blogger or WordPress account to get started; the rest is rather easy. Just keep in mind two things: You need to have something valuable to say or show off, and you need to post regularly to keep visitors returning for more. Opening up the posts to comments is a great way to connect with others and spark lively discussions. Share posts on social media or submit guest posts to bigger blogs in order to get the word out about yours. Once a blog is established, you can make additional money by offering courses and posting ads from sponsors on it the way Andrea Scher does at *www.superherolife.com.*

Of course, you'll want your blog to center around a concept. Maybe you're an artist who combs the Web for cool resources and samples of delectable designs. A writer may offer tips on writing or interview other writers. Some people turn to blogging as a full-time career, but you don't have to make it your mainstay to do well at it.

Must-Reads

Blogging for Creatives: How Designers, Artists, Crafters and Writers Can Blog to Make Contacts, Win Business and Build Success **by Robin Houghton and** *Blog, Inc.: Blogging for Passion, Profit, and to Create Communit* **by Meg Mateo Ilasco and Joy Deangdeelert Cho**

Alternative Revenue Stream #4: Make Sound Waves: Podcast!

If writing isn't for you, maybe you're looking for another way to spread your creative wings.

I began podcasting on Freelance Radio a few years back, and the experience has been beyond rewarding. I receive countless e-mails stating that the tips and stories I have shared helped others. And to boot, I've landed some pretty cool gigs across the globe thanks to the exposure.

Starting a podcast isn't as easy as it sounds. You need the right technologies in place aside from a computer with a microphone. When I podcast, it is just as a panelist; I never did any of the tech work. Freelance Radio was only possible because Dickie Adams did all the sound and recording "stuff" behind the scenes. Even Von Glitschka contributed to designing a logo. I simply participated in the discussions. Like Corey Feldman in the film *The Goonies,* I was the "mouth" of the operation.

If you have fresh ideas for a show, and, like blogging, you can commit regularly to podcasting, this can be a wonderful way to position yourself as a thought leader in the creative industry. People new to freelancing are looking to connect with others in their shoes and get valuable tips on staying in business. Newbies and veterans alike appreciate the information and likely make awesome guests as well.

At the time I was writing this book, Freelance Radio was on a hiatus, but I am hoping the show is back and running by the time you read this. You can check out our archive of episodes at *www.freelanceradio. com* or find the show on iTunes. I promise that, if nothing else, it will entertain you. (And you'll be able to laugh at my "Joisey" accent!)

Resource
Listen to podcasts on freelance life at *www.freelanceradio.com,* *www.freelancejam.com,* *www.freelanceadvisor.co.uk,* *www.freelancefolder.com,* **and** *www.thedeependdesign.com.*

Alternate Revenue Stream #5: Teach

Another way to advance yourself professionally involves sharing your insights and giving others instruction on how to develop their talents and professional aptitudes. A freelancer friend of mine has begun to work with an educational company teaching others about illustration and design techniques. I know another solo-pro who develops courses in photography and personal growth, and promotes them on her blog.

Another avenue for teaching is to approach trade organizations and companies with a course idea. Several of the Web sites you turn to for industry information offer valuable classes that you can take—and teach. Going to your local university, community college, or community education program is also a fantastic idea if you want to explore teaching.

Using Your Creative Edge to Develop Yourself Professionally

You'll notice that these five revenue streams are often used interchangeably among many veteran freelancers, though some only focus on one. Starting out as a rookie, you may be focused solely on building your business, which is a good idea. As time goes on and you gain some expertise, though, you may want to contemplate expanding your platform.

All of these are fabulous ways to make some extra moolah based on your talent and cultivate it at the same time. The key is finding out which ones encompass your creative edge. If writing isn't your thing, you may not want to consider writing a book. But if it's something you have always wanted to do and you think you have something insightful to say, go for it.

Alternative revenue streams require passion because they come secondary to your business, so make sure you have the devotion and enthusiasm needed to sustain them. At the end of the day, these may require more work, but they can go a long way to make your career more fulfilling, bolster your brand, and, in turn, help you land even more clients.

Sweet Success
A Passion for Helping Freelancers

In 2003, Julie Cortés had been plugging along as a freelance copywriter for half a decade when she formed the Freelance Exchange of Kansas City (*www.kcfreelanceexchange.com*). Cortés formed the group because she believes that freelancers often deal with the same issues yet never share them. She thought, "Why don't we swap notes with one another on what works and what doesn't, and if we don't have the answers, we'll bring in an expert to teach us?"

Not only is the organization (*www.kcfreelanceexchange.com*) helpful for building a network, the group hosts an annual portfolio showcase and an awards show. Cortés wanted more, however, so she developed a business plan for Freelancers University.

"With this concept, I realized I could get back to my true love of educating other freelancers," she says. "Freelancers U was born to offer individuals an opportunity to master the fine art of being self-employed. It essentially picks up where your formal education left off... you can discover all the little nuances it takes to start, run, and succeed in the wonderful world of freelancing."

Beginner Mishap
Stumbling Over Oneself

When copywriter Alexandra Franzen (*www.alexandrafranzen.com*) first launched her professional writing business, she knew that she wasn't sure who she was, or who she was becoming. She attended a few networking events for guidance.

At events, others would ask her, "So what do you do?" That's when the Minnesota-based writer was at a loss for words. "I'd freeze like a startled rabbit, rack my brain for the most appropriate answer, and then sputter out something dull, vague, or simply bewildering," recalls Franzen, who believes her mistake was pretending to have a polished job title and introduction. "I was moving through a necessary, brave, and undeniably *awkward* growth spurt. If I could swoosh back in time, I would've honored and owned my awkwardness, instead of trying to unsuccessfully mask it."

Her lesson to others who are just figuring out their business and how to develop professional skills is to be honest, humble, and human, "whether you're at the top of your game—or figuring out what your game is in the first place."

Chapter 10

Long-Term Talent

Remember the business blueprint we discussed all the way back in Chapter 2? Now may be a good time to dig it out. Up until now, we've talked about how to start and operate a business. But how will you make it work after you devise an accounting system, launch your Web site, and secure a couple of gigs?

Make it Work

A few years ago, one of my good friends I knew during college began freelancing. John Mitchell (*www.jmitchellproductions.blogspot. com*), whom you met in Chapter 5, went from being a mortgage loan officer to a videographer—and he hasn't looked back since he took the plunge. "Like a lot of things, the first few jobs were for peanuts or even nothing, but once I got the experience...bigger and more expensive jobs came my way," says Mitchell, who lives in New Jersey. "Once you get the ball rolling, you start meeting other people interested in your work and it just keeps going in like a revolving door with more people giving you work and you delivering the work at the same time."

The fact that Mitchell is *the single funniest person I know* is, I think, a large part of his success. Earlier in the book, I talked about how he used his vivacious personality to connect with clients via cold-calling. His personality allures clients, but it's also key to retaining them.

Cracking a good joke may not sound like much of a competitive edge, but for Mitchell, his persona has been paramount to his accomplishments as a creative. He's been in business for several years now, so I'd say it has been a huge advantage.

What has been working for your business? Consistently evaluate what's effective and go with it, then toss out what is not. You'll need to do this throughout your career as the market changes and your abilities evolve.

Kill 'Em With Kindness—Even When You Wanna Kill 'Em

You can churn out stellar work, meet deadlines, publish, and speak at conferences across the globe. To be a true success, though, you also have to be, well, *nice.*

That's what Jim Kraus (*www.jimkrausdesign.com*) says. The designer, illustrator, photographer, and author from Washington insists that being kind is imperative. It doesn't mean that you have to make all sorts of compromises to satisfy a client; it simply means that you have to do like your momma said and be pleasant.

Whether things are going great or going south, it's still important to be friendly to clients. No matter what you have to say to a client, I guarantee you it can be said kindly—even if you are ending the relationship. "Talented and courteous creative professionals are almost always chosen over talented and unpleasant creative professionals," Kraus says.

If you find yourself in a cranky mood and have to deal with a client, try your best to put on a happy face or voice. You can always recite your favorite four-letter word after the call or meeting is over, but for a little bit, it's better to take the agreeable route.

Thriving in Your Work Environment

Your work environment also contributes to how well you do as a freelancer. If I was still in a cubicle under fluorescent lighting working from 8 to 5—even if I was writing best-sellers every day—I would have been out of business a long time ago!

On any given day, you can find me working just about anywhere. From my local coffeehouse to my living room couch, I like to change up my atmosphere depending on my mood or the project. I think having different settings for work can make tasks more enjoyable.

I know people who run profitable businesses in their PJs, and I also hear from others that have to get dressed in the morning and can only work in their home office. Some freelancers prefer to work from a studio or office, which can enhance productivity, offer a neutral meeting place, and lend a more credible feel to business.

What steps have you taken to make your personal work space work best for you?

"I have a home office that I like to work out of when I'm not out shooting or meeting with clients. I like it to be quiet for the most part, and I have room darkening shades for when I'm retouching images on the computer."

—Carey Kirkella, lifestyle/portrait photographer,
www.careykirkella.com

Christine Mason Miller (*www.christinemasonmiller.com*), a California-based artist and author who has freelanced for more than 15 years, has rented studio space in the past. She said the venue made it easier to engage in her creative work. Another perk: She could leave it a mess at the end of the day and go home to her clean house. These days, she has an office in her house, but admits it does present some distractions.

I work from home. I have never wanted to have an office mainly because I want to keep my overhead low, plus I didn't want to have to *go* to work each day. Sometimes when I feel like I have cabin fever, I either take a break during the day to do something else or bring my laptop to either the library or a coffeehouse. Switching up your work environment makes you more productive and can help break through creative blocks.

I would definitely say that I take better care of my home because I want it to be an inspiring, relaxing work environment. Also, I have a laptop and desktop, so when I don't feel like being chained to my desk, I can go mobile to the patio, the couch, or my bed. I have learned to let myself take advantage of all the perks that come with self-employment.

If your business reaches the point that you feel the need to work outside your home office, you may want to consider renting studio space. You may also want to think about a short-term rental so you can get a feel for it before you commit to something on a long-term basis.

Growing out of Your PJs: Expanding Your Enterprise

In thinking about where you want to go with your business and where you want your business to go, you have probably considered whether or not to expand it.

Being able to grow into a firm or agency is a measure of success, but that's not to say that those who do not pursue a larger entity are not prosperous. It depends what you want out of your business. Obviously there are pros and cons to these options.

I know a few entrepreneurs that enjoyed using their talent when they started as a solo professional, but found increased gratification by expanding their operation into a company. Maybe you will find that you enjoy sales and want to drive more of a client's strategy more than the actual design, development, production, crafting, or writing.

Just keep in mind as you go what you want your business to become as it grows, because it will prosper if you put your all into it. If you elect to stay solo, you'll have to manage your workload so you can keep your fingertips on every aspect of business to maintain its boutique nature.

Ditching Your Home Office for a Client's Pad

Another aspect of your long-term success as a freelancer can involve working for clients on-site, either by offering to travel to their office or accepting temporary contracts through creative agencies. We will focus on agencies because that's the most popular form of on-site work. (Most freelancers, when they find they can work from home, never want to head back to an office.)

I know freelancers who don't mind going into the office now and then, and others that avoid it the way a vampire shies away from daylight. Working for a client at their office is something to contemplate when you think about the clients you want to attract. You may start off taking on-site gigs and decide as you obtain more clients that being in someone else's workspace isn't your cup of tea.

Working on-site for a creative firm (or even for a client directly) doesn't make you any less of a freelancer. I think it makes you smart because it keeps money coming in, lowers overhead costs, and can offer you access to work on brands that you may not otherwise have had the chance to work for. It can provide a reliable paycheck, too, because most of the jobs last a few weeks or months.

Another plus to working on-site is that a company may retain you for more projects, or for a full-time position. This would be an ideal situation if you discover that freelancing isn't for you and are looking to segue back into a traditional job.

"Freelancers seeking a staff role should do their best to impress the bosses, and should also be explicit in explaining this desire," advises Prescott Perez-Fox (*www.strshp.com*), an art director and graphic designer from New Jersey. "Otherwise, bosses will assume you enjoy freelancing and will pass you over when they are recruiting for full-timers."

A good idea is to touch base with creative agencies and inform them as your availability changes. If you're in the middle of a slump and a project is up for grabs, taking it may help you stay on your feet financially. Having agency work prospects is a good idea to keep work coming in as you build your client base.

How can you leverage connections and clips from on-site work for your business?

"Much like you should never work with a client of your own without a contract or agreement, you should always make sure to sign some kind of contractor agreement or privacy policy, usually supplied by the client. There's almost always a segment about work rights and ownership, which translates to the portfolio. Chances are you'll be able to show projects in your portfolio after the work goes public, and with due credit to the agency who employed you at the time. Often, the client will specify that you can't display the work publicly, as on your website or submitted for a contest, but you can show the work in the privacy of an interview. It's a grey area in many cases."

—Prescott Perez-Fox, art director/graphic designer, *www.strshp.com*

Resource

Do a Google search for "coworking" along with the state, region, or city you live in. Visit *www.deskmag.com*, an online magazine devoted to coworking, and *www.coworking.com*, a community for coworking.

Feast or Famine

The concept of *feast or famine* seems to be a popular struggle for many solo-pros. Just about every freelancer out there—if not all of them—are familiar with the concept of being desperate for work or too overloaded to breathe. Even though things ebb and flow for seasoned freelancers, they tend to deal with those ups and downs a little more naturally. Why? After a while, and only after you have lived through it, you see that things equalize, especially if you are doing all you can to control your business.

As a newbie freelancer, I would hit highs when I had more work than I knew what to do with, but I would also feel depressed and blame myself personally when I wasn't working 40 hours a week. I was lucky enough that my husband gently reminded me each time work was slow, "You went through this before, remember? It always turns out all right."

It took me a while to gain some clarity during famines. The truth is, most of my famines wouldn't even qualify as a famine. I would panic after a slow week and then be bombarded the next. This is a good thing; I know that many self-employed people go through longer bouts without incoming projects.

Nowadays, I struggle more with having too much work on my plate, rather than not having enough. That certainly doesn't mean I haven't had my fair share slow times. Talking myself through the famines has gotten much easier, but it honestly took me a few years to trust my business. Now I know that when work is slow, it's not my fault; it's just how it is. Plus, I've learned to channel some of my negative thinking into securing more projects. In fact, I do some of my best marketing when I know that I need to bring in more clients stat.

Freelancers talk about the famine all the time, but I don't think they recognize the *challenges* that can come with the feast.

A few years back, a client offered me what I like to refer to as a "whopper" project: I was going to write content for not one, but nearly a dozen Web sites. These weren't little mamas, either; each Web site was worth a few thousand dollars. I tried to clear my schedule as much as possible to accommodate the enormous workload and tight deadlines. Though I will always be grateful for the project—that puppy paid more than a few bills—it did teach me a valuable lesson: Feasting can be just as tough as going through a famine, specifically when you have a Type A personality like I do.

As freelancers, it's difficult to admit that there are negatives to every situation, even if it's a great experience overall. We may feel like we are not entitled to feel overwhelmed because we are living our dreams. You may not want to complain if you're over-the-top busy with a project, or if you get the opportunity to work for a high-profile client, but you also have to give yourself permission to feel whatever you feel. The greatest opportunities can also present some of the toughest times for a solo-pro. Keeping your eye on the prize, in those cases, is your best defense; ultimately something good will come out of a feast, but that doesn't mean it cannot be a trying time for you.

Even though I was thrilled to take on the whopper project, taking care of myself became my top priority during that time. I tried to eat as well as possible, and even when I thought I didn't have time to make it to the gym, I still went. Sometimes you have to go into survival mode when you're feasting; you have to power through. That doesn't mean you can't take care of yourself.

While I was writing this book, I went into a feast mode. (You know, every client wants something done when you *finally* get that book deal!) Even though it was stressful and forced me to skip out on a more than a few beach days, writing this book was still an awesome experience to say the least!

My point is that you can be starving for work and miserable—or have more projects than you know what to do with and still be peeved. The key is to learn to be content whether your in-box is brimming with messages or just plain empty. Take the time to acknowledge and work through your feelings. The next time things are challenging, it will probably be easier to deal with. You will build up confidence in your ability to thrive no matter what arises. I think the only way you can learn is by drawing upon the things that get you through the famines and the feasts, and seeing that you can overcome them time and again.

Steady and Sustainable

One of the best ways to combat famines is to hold down some sort of steady job when you freelance. I'm not talking about taking a part-time gig that has nothing to do with your creative talent. What I mean is securing some sort of steady or regular work so you don't have to rely on random projects trickling in. Sure, veterans may not have to do it, but until you can cultivate that strong base of clients, you may need to make ends meet, and this is a good way to do it!

There are a few tricks to snagging steady work. Again, a repeat client or steady gig doesn't make you any less of a freelancer; they just help your business remain stable. In fact, I know many solo-pros that only work with a select few clients and derive most of their profits from just a few gigs because they know that a flowing pipeline of work means more time with their talent and less time processing contracts and payments.

I like the hybrid approach. I recently took on a part-time gig with regular hours. I also have a solid base of various clients that provide ongoing work. Throughout it all, I take on clients that only use my services once. These multiple pipelines of work have kept me busy and paid regularly.

Let's face it: Marketing your business is vital, but eventually, you may not want to rely on having to constantly sell your services. (That doesn't mean you shouldn't market yourself regularly, though.) It can take a few years to have a referral-driven business, and even experienced solo-pros that receive the majority of their projects from referrals still need to keep up with self-promotion. In holding down one or a few clients with ongoing projects, this lets you outreach to new ones while having a somewhat-steady paycheck. My regular clients may not feed me a project every week or every month, but I know when they need assistance writing they turn to me. This, along with one-time clients, seems to be a winning formula for me.

The type of clients you have will change as you go, but as you become more experienced, you will have more of a say in your client base. I always want new clients, but I like having a few regulars as well. It keeps money coming in so I can afford to grow the arm of my business dedicated to book and magazine writing. Whatever you decide, again, keep in mind to think about what types of clients you want as you go. Through time, you will be able to realize the vision with a mix of clients that suits you best.

Goal Setting

In Chapter 2, we talked about the concept of business planning and you (hopefully) created a business blueprint. Goal setting is another vital component that successful freelancers deploy to keep business booming. Usually this is most popular around the New Year because just about everyone is setting resolutions or vowing to improve upon things. As a business owner, however, you need to be constantly conceiving aspirations and revisiting your business strategy.

Breaking down your goals is key. Instead of just saying "I'm going to make enough money as a freelancer this year to support myself," try thinking in terms of what you need to break down that goal into easily manageable steps. Maybe you need to earn a definite amount of money per month to pay the bills. From there, you may go on to say that you want to work on a specific number of projects that will help you earn that amount. When you simplify goals into baby steps, you're more likely to achieve them—plus, breaking it down can make the big picture seem a little less daunting.

In a few Freelance Radio episodes, I spoke about my desire to write more for magazines. Dickie Adams helped me simplify my goal of "getting published more in magazines" into an attainable task; we agreed that I would send out a certain number of pitch letters per week or per month. Armed with a renewed sense of motivation, I began to send those letters.

See, magazine article writing takes time. The ideas you pitch may be awesome, but an editor may not want them at the time due to a number of factors. So, saying I would publish an article a month or something to that end could realistically be unattainable because the choice to publish an article is not in my hands. The choice to query magazines, however, was. In setting the goal to put letters out, I put my ideas out there. If I got an article assignment but it didn't publish for six months or a year, that was all right. In breaking down the goal into something I could control, I accomplished it.

Now, I regularly block off time to query even when I have work to fixate on. In doing so, I continuously secure assignments. One month, I had two magazine articles on the shelves at the same time. (Of course I took pictures of them at Barnes and Noble!)

How can I secure commissioned work for my photos and artwork?

"Keep in touch with people who show an interest in your work and be sure to update them periodically on anything new that you've done and you're proud of. Be professional and friendly in all of your communication with prospective clients, and try to create more personal relationships with them. When you do get a commissioned assignment, deliver great quality work and be pleasant to work with. That will obviously help you get more work in the future, either through them or through referrals."

—Carey Kirkella, lifestyle/portrait photographer,
www.careykirkella.com

Must-Read
The Artist's Way **by Julia Cameron**

Creative Blocks—and Creative Bricks

When the creative juices stop flowing for solo-pros, it can be more than annoying; it can possibly damage your career. If you procrastinate like most people, a time crunch can add even more pressure when you are scraping for ideas.

The most common creative block occurs when you cannot dream up a creative idea; say, if you have to write a tagline or originate a new design. Other matters that impact your imagination include going through a personal or emotional issue.

I hear from a lot of solo-pros that battle creative blocks. I think the remedy is to *stop trying so hard* when they are feeling creatively barren. For me, a drive to Starbucks for a grandé skim no-water chai tea, or simply focusing on another task—sometimes, even housework—is useful. That's why it is a good idea to avoid tight deadlines and procrastination: You never know if you're going to need that time to get unblocked.

I realize that it may be easier for me to overcome a block than others, but definitely try new techniques to combat your next creative block. Fighting it, moping about it, or posting a whiny Facebook status will do little to make the situation better. Instead, try a different physical activity, take a break or a vacation, spend the afternoon out of the office, or experiment with another creative medium.

When I was connecting with creatives to write this book, I connected with a freelance journalist in New York that put a name to a signature issue that creatives grapple with that is similar to the idea of creative blocks—but opposite. Janene Mascarella (*www.janenemascarella.com*) frequently deals with what she calls writer's brick, a completely made-up condition when you have too many ideas instead of not enough. I loved the concept; I hadn't thought of it, so I wanted to mention it.

"*Writer's brick* is when you get slapped upside the head with so many article ideas that you become completely overwhelmed," explains

Mascarella. "You are quietly researching a topic or writing an article, when—*whammo!*—out of nowhere you are suddenly slammed with incredible ideas. One after the other, until everything goes fuzzy." She says the trick to overcome writer's brick is to ease up on the multitasking. "Doing too much at once may be trendy but it's not productive at all," Mascarella says.

I think what Mascarella says is so important because there are two sides to every conundrum. Sometimes it's not just about writer's block, sometimes it's a brick that hits you. The same way that the whole feast-or-famine syndrome is just about dealing with the buffet as it is about starvation.

Resource

Check out *www.creativeclearinghouse.com, www.howdesign.com, www.creativesuccess.com/blog,* *www.juliacameronlive.com,* **or** *www.illustrationclass.com.*

The Key to Productivity: Getting Into "the Zone"

One would think that the threat of not keeping income flowing in would be reason enough to get busy, but the truth is that sustaining productivity can be hard for solo-pros. If you moonlight, it's difficult to come home after a full day of work and devote time to your freelance business. Working efficiently can be a challenge because we shift gears often, going from different projects to business administration tasks while responding to phone calls and e-mails—and trying to do it all while working with our natural creative highs and lows. Even though I'm not a procrastinator, I do struggle to be productive some days. I also find it hard to dive back into work after I finish a long-term project, or after I am interrupted.

I like what Alexandra Franzen (*www.alexandrafranzen.com*), a copywriter based in Minnesota, says about productivity. She believes it's a matter of falling into your *creative rhythm.* "Once I discovered my creative rhythm, and started to design my life and business in *accordance* with it—instead of *against* it—my entire world upleveled," Franzen says. Her attitude shifted and her income tripled.

To do this, she says you must detect times when you're in "the zone," that place where you don't feel like you're laboring and you don't want to take a break from what you're doing. Other symptoms of this phenomenon for me include forgetting to eat and seeing an hour flash by in what feels like 10 minutes.

To identify when you are in the zone, she says to remember what you were doing when you forgot to eat lunch or the afternoon seemed to whiz by. For instance, I don't always get into the zone when I'm doing a copywriting project, but I'm almost always at a place of nirvana when I'm writing a magazine article. Time flies. "Moments of ease, fluidity, and sensational productivity are major clues to your creative rhythm," Franzen notes.

Do you get into the zone during a specific time of day? Or does being at a certain location help you tune in? If your happiness is contingent on the activity you're doing, you will tend to focus on the talent-related work instead of mundane-but-necessary tasks—and that can be a killer for your biz. Instead, accomplishing the things you are less thrilled about when you are at your peak focus time is key. Then, even if you're not at your peak, you will likely look forward to the creative tasks with a sense of renewed energy.

If you can't get into the zone when you're doing what you love, you may not be in the right career. Play around a little; you may have to tweak where you work or find clients you like more to find a good tempo. For instance, I typically handle administrative tasks at my desk in the middle of the day, while I reserve working on my laptop on the patio, in bed, or in my living room for tasks I enjoy more. When I'm really in the zone, however, I can sit at my desk for hours and not feel that I'm working at all.

"Aim for a resentment-free schedule, and you'll be 10 strides closer to your ideal creative rhythm," Franzen says.

My top productivity tip is to know and listen to your body. For example, I work best either first thing in the morning or in the afternoon. A typical day for me involves waking up and either working for a bit or going directly to the gym, then coming home to continue working. It's best for me to complete tasks I don't particularly enjoy during my peak productivity times because I have the energy to tackle them. I get another burst of energy after finishing, and I can move on to my creative work.

To find your creative pulse, pay attention to the times you shine and pick up on those instances. This isn't to say that you can't be productive when you are doing something you don't enjoy or when your energy is zapped. Just listen to yourself. Inside, we all know what we need and how to best maneuver in life.

Resource
View some productivity tools at *www.modernfreelance.com, www.creativefreelancerblog.com,* and *www.zenhabits.com*.

What's the key to long-term success as a freelancer?

"Trust your intuition. Work hard. Embrace that this journey will be an interplay between your visions and other possibilities you can't yet envision. Consider your dream an entity that you are building a partnership with. Trust it, let it lead you."

—Christine Mason Miller, artist/writer,
www.christinemasonmiller.com

Reaching Out

Rome wasn't built in a day. Nurturing your growing business will certainly take time. One way to speed up that process is to ask for guidance.

That doesn't mean you have to directly ask others for assistance, though I think many people in the creative community will offer theirs. You can also gain assistance and knowledge by staying on top of the industry. Read magazines or attend a seminar. Scroll through on-line forums. Nurture connections you make via networking—even if it's only on-line.

My Twitter followers know that I have no problem asking for assistance. During the time I was writing this book and looking for interviewees, I was never shy about putting a post out asking for my tweeples to scrounge their networks for sources I could interview. So many people were responsive and obliging; I connected with numerous solo-pros that I never would have encountered had I not asked for assistance.

Whether you are in a conundrum with a client or simply want to grasp a new technology used in your field, that network can be instrumental. Then, whenever you have questions, ask away! I guarantee you that others you connect with are bound to offer up their expertise and support. Creatives are cool like that!

Setting the Tone for a Thriving Freelance Business

Remember: Freelancing isn't a cookie-cutter career. What works for one person does not work for all. You probably got into freelancing so you could do your own thing, and that's exactly what you need to do in order to excel. Eventually, it becomes easier to trust your intuition. "Nobody knows what's going to work for you...emphasis on *you*. Nobody can tell you—with absolute, iron-clad, you-can-bank-on-it certainty how to make your video go viral, how to guarantee that your campaign is a starry-eyed success, how to get your book on the bestseller list..." says Franzen. "All anybody can do is tell you what worked for them, what's proven for others and likely for some."

Franzen jokes, "All you can do is throw hot spaghetti at the wall and see what sticks, what falls to the floor and what makes you smile." I like Franzen's analogy, not only because I am textbook Italian and enjoy carbs; it's good because freelancing is kind of a gamble. That doesn't mean your success is out of your control; it means you don't know what will happen next or how to approach different situations until you face them head-on.

That's the good thing about having your talent. Chances are, the world will benefit from the natural gifts you have to share. And with some business know-how under your belt, well, now you stand even more of a chance to succeed. In fact, I think you're kind of unstoppable.

Sweet Success
A Tear-Jerker
        When Luke Mysse (*www.lukemysse.com*) was asked to speak at HOW's Creative Freelancer Conference, he was shocked and gladly accepted. When he got up to speak, he was following a well-known speaker. "Nobody knew who I was," says Mysse, of California. Still, his presentation was a hit because his authentic approach resonated with the audience.

Although he felt vulnerable during his speech, he wound up feeling a little more emotional than normal after he stepped off the stage and mingled with conference participants.

Later on, he returned to his hotel room, thinking about the journey he had taken from running his business to being an industry speaker, and feeling proud. It was impressive, so he was confused when he started crying.

Wondering where the waterworks were coming from, Mysse spotted his thyroid medication on the dresser. He realized he had forgotten to take the medication, which, if not taken on time, can cause hormonal haywire. "I was like, 'Wow, I shouldn't be crying like this,'" he laughs.

Mysse was excited about his experience but giggles when he thinks about how emotional he got. True, he spoke from his heart, but the crying was a little too much—even for him. To date, Mysse hasn't shed any tears at a speaking event, but he looks back on his presentation and says he is pretty sure he was the only one moved to tears.

Beginner Mishap
Trust Is Vital for Project Collaboration

When Grace Smith (*www.postscript5.co.uk*), an Ireland-based Web designer, began moonlighting, she took on a rather large project and hired a developer to take on some of the workload. They agreed on specs and pricing, but never signed a contract. "However, when it came time for the developer to hand over the files he had been working on, I couldn't get hold of him," she recalls. "He hadn't been paid, so it wasn't a case of him running away with the cash, either."

Smith was frantic. "Here I was ready to launch this site, without the necessary files and a developer that had gone AWOL," she says. "It was the worst moment in my freelance career...then and since."

Smith snapped into action to find another developer, who finished the project quickly and did a better job than the first guy. In the end, the project was delayed, but the client was happy.

"As a freelance creative, trust is key," explains Smith. "When you subcontract work, you are entrusting your business—and reputation—to that person, so be sure they are a true professional and value high standards as much as you do."

Chapter 11

Business on the Side

My poor little moonlighters. Did you really need to read the whole book in order to help you run a thriving freelance business? Couldn't you just have skipped to this chapter and taken what you needed from it?

Nope. (Even if you're not a moonlighter or never were, you should read this chapter because it contains useful information for all freelancers.)

Moonlighters, who work full-time jobs in addition to running a business on the side, still need to understand all the vital components of operating a business. From knowing how to market yourself to understanding taxes, you will manage your business just about the same way as a full-time freelancer. The difference is that you'll hold down a full-time job while you do it!

When it comes to moonlighting, the concept of working a side job runs the gamut. Some pursue a hobby on the side and use it to make extra cash. Others are so miserable in their 9-to-5 jobs that freelancing is the only way to feel fulfilled. Many people are happy in their traditional jobs; they just like having a secondary business. I believe that most creatives, however, would like to turn a side gig into their full-time one.

Moonlighting can be a wonderful way to explore the business possibilities that can come from your natural artistic talent. I was able to moonlight for about two years until I built up my business and could "swim" financially in order to go solo. Your goal may be not to run your own business full-time, so moonlighting may be the perfect way to apply your creative gift. Again, you still have to know the basics of running a business—even if it's not on a full-time basis!

Some might insist that a side business is not as legitimate as one that's a full-time deal. Nonsense! Even if they are not available to their clients during regular business hours because they are employed, moonlighters can still operate a solid enterprise.

 Must-Read
Escape from Cubicle Nation: From Corporate Prisoner to Thriving Entrepreneur **by Pamela Slim**

Moonlighting by the Numbers

Did you know that one in 17 Americans hold down multiple jobs? According to the U.S. Department of Labor, anywhere from seven to eight million Americans—5 percent of all workers—work more than one gig, according to the *Los Angeles Times*. You can bet that number grew when the economy tanked a few years ago. In 2011, 543,000 Americans started a business each month, the 2012 Freelance Industry Report states. That same report notes "According to a May 2012 Aberdeen Group report, in the U.S. alone nearly 26 percent of the average organization's total workforce is considered contingent or contract based, and their numbers continue to grow rapidly" and that "labor law firm Littler Midelson predicts that contingent labor could rise to as much as 30 percent to 50 percent of the entire U.S. workforce over the next few years."

In fact, if you began freelancing as a result of a layoff—you're also known as an "accidental freelancer"—you typically earn less than those that planned their self-employment. Even though accidental freelancers may not earn as much as "intentional freelancers," 51.5 percent of them claim they are happier working solo, according to the report. Still, 55 percent of them report they would likely accept a traditional employment if given the chance. Only 38 percent of traditional freelancers say they would consider kissing their solo careers goodbye.

The report also states that finding clients is the biggest challenge for accidental freelancers, probably because traditional freelancers likely had time to plan their escapes from the corporate grind; accidentals are tossed into it.

There are many reasons to start moonlighting. In the creative arena, it's predominantly to pursue your passion full- or part-time. In doing do, my hope is that you run a business that financially supports you *and* fulfills you.

Pros and Cons

Having a secondary career comes with advantages and disadvantages. A few of the pros include being able to do the following:

→ **Try your hand at a creative calling.** If you've always wanted to be an animator but didn't want to leave the stability of your 9-to-5 job, a creative side business lets you to put your talents in motion.

→ **Enjoy all the perks of a traditional job and live your dream.** When you moonlight, you can reap the glory of a regular paycheck, healthcare plan, and other benefits. This gives you the time to develop your business and not worry too much about pulling in a certain amount of money. This is particularly valuable if you have a family to support because it gives you the means to make a gradual shift into self-employment or simply enjoy juggling both jobs.

→ **Hand-pick clients.** When you do not have to live off your talent, you may be more likely to cherry-pick the clients you want—and deal with a lot less drama than someone who depends on not-so-awesome clients to stay afloat.

→ **See if you can build up enough customers to go solo.** I would say the biggest advantage to moonlighting is that you may be able to turn it into a full-time career. If you have that dream of "going solo," moonlighting offers the perfect middle ground to help you do so.

With that, there are some drawbacks associated with moonlighting:

→ **Doing business during business hours.** Perhaps your traditional job requires you to be there during regular business hours. That can put a huge damper on a client who wants to have a mid-day conference call.

→ **Managing your time.** Obviously, juggling two jobs is hard because you probably have multiple obligations that can include a family. One job is hard enough; no one says working two is easy.

→ **Disclosure issues.** It is hard for many freelancers to decide if they should tell their bosses about their side business. If it's in a similar field, the boss may be leery that you may snag their customers. Even if not, a supervisor may be more vigilant if he suspects you may be working on his clock. (If you have an exceptionally boring job with plenty of spare time, it's tough not to occupy yourself with activities related to your side gig—but that can spell trouble if your boss doesn't give you the okay first.)

→ **Starving your potential.** I know a few freelancers that are beyond capable of running a full-time business but don't because the security of a regular job is so comfortable—and stepping out of that comfort zone is not.

Why have you decided to continue moonlighting instead of pursuing self-employment?

"Benefits and pay, primarily. Having solid insurance coverage makes a big difference when you have a growing family. Paid vacation is also a nice perk. I still enjoy expanding my professional horizons, which is why I even moonlight or freelance at all. For larger projects, I do try to push work to fellow freelancers who work full-time at their chosen career."

—Dickie Adams, designer,
www.dickieadams.com

Are You Freelancing Aimlessly?

I'm not sure if it's a blessing or a curse. That is, some creatives who moonlight either don't have to be concerned or blatantly don't care if they are conducting business ethically or even turning a profit. Some are simply moonlighting for the enjoyment of it—not to mention the opportunity for *extra* cash; really, there is nothing wrong with that. But if you want to turn your side gig into self-employment, you definitely need to be planning for it—not wandering haphazardly.

In writing this book, I interviewed a 20-something who used *www.etsy.com* to sell her crafts. She claimed her marketing platform was to "basically" get herself "out there" without investing any money in her business. This young woman filled orders for her crafts, but wasn't working to generate leads or build up a client base. The year before, she wasn't even sure if she earned a profit. This is an example of someone I would refer to as an *aimless freelancer.* I think aimless freelancing is more common among moonlighters, but I am sure there are many full-timers that fit the bill. In her case, she's probably just enjoying a *hobby* but when she starts earning money off it and providing professional services, it needs to be run like a *business.*

Is there anything wrong with this type of person? Of course not. She can do whatever she wants. I used her as an example because it is a smart idea to think about the type of moonlighter you want to be. Do you want to have a hobby, or will you make your hobby a business?

You'll have to do a few things like pay taxes, create a Web presence, cultivate relationships with clients, and protect yourself from legal issues. Perhaps you don't have to work on finding the bacon if you're not going to rely on the enterprise financially, but otherwise, you'll need to run a business.

So, are you an aimless freelancer? I doubt it. I like to think that if you picked up this book, you're not careless at all. In fact, you're on the right path if you are taking charge of your business.

What type of business planning did you do before starting your full-time creative business?

"When I was moonlighting, I only had business cards and I used a Yahoo account for e-mail. When I decided to become a business, I held focus groups to create a title for the company. Then, I researched and took classes on the various types of companies. Once we had the list of company names narrowed down, I called the state to see which ones were available for an LLC. I obtained my LLC and Employer Identification Number (EIN) and then opened a business checking account with this information. I then transferred my e-mail over to look more professional and put up a small Web site."

—April Michelle Davis, editor/indexer/proofreader,
www.editorialinspirations.com

One Person, Two Very Different Careers

Aside from the aimless freelancer, there are other types of moonlighters. Some have a side business in the same profession that they hold a full-time job in (as would an art director with a freelance graphic design business), but others feel as if they are living truly double lives because their freelance business is so different from their day job. I like to call them *right-side-left-side freelancers,* meaning they may work in a technical or left-brain career. On the flip side, their creative business ignites the right side—the creative side—of the brain.

I did that dance when I worked in a 9-to-5 job in the environmental field as a technical writer and would come home to work on sales-y marketing copy at night. The dichotomy of working in a technical field while using my creative talents after-hours was the impetus for me to go freelance. It was nice because I always looked forward to the end of the day when I could go home and get artsy, but I found it frustrating to spend more than eight hours a day doing something that was not nearly as enjoyable.

Lori Riviere, a blogger, stylist, and personal shopper from Miami, is leading that sort of double life—and loving it. Her blog (*www.shortcut-stofabulous.com*) offers up fashion, beauty, and lifestyle tips and tricks for women. When she's not busy with her Web site, she's working full-time as an attorney for one of the largest insurance companies in the country. When she first developed the concept for the blog, she was working at a private law firm, which required 60- to 70-hour workweeks.

"I knew that as long as I was working for this firm, I would never be able to make my dreams to have a creative outlet outside of the law a reality," recalls Riviere. "I was working crazy hours...and I was miserable." In order to pursue her aspirations to be both a blogger and stylist, she needed a different full-time job as an attorney that would give her more flexibility. Riviere secured a full-time job as a lawyer that required less time, and then began to develop her Web site.

It took more than a year to get everything rolling because she had to do much more than get a domain name and start writing. Riviere's secured advertisers for her blog, fostered partnerships to offer her readers discounts, and built up a solid reputation in the fashion and lifestyle blogging arena. While she's been at it, she's also picked up fashion styling clients in the Miami area, which mostly comes from word-of-mouth and referrals.

"I started taking my friends out shopping to build their wardrobes. They kept telling me that I should do this for a living," she recalls. "So I spent $20 on business cards and gave them to my friends." That's how she built up clientele for her creative business.

Though she's still dispensing legal advice, Riviere is enjoying her "double life" as a legalista and fashionista, though she admits balancing both is not always easy.

One thing that helps her is having a very supportive boss. "He often brags about my double life when we run into people in the legal community," she notes. Even though she's dying to find out about the latest designer handbag and shoe deals—and even more eager to pass them on to her growing readership base of approximately 3,000 monthly visitors—Riviere keeps busy with court appearance and depositions by day.

She says it can be difficult to schedule time to interview people for her blog, make television and radio appearances, and coordinate appointments with clients for styling and personal shopping. "The other day, I ended up doing a radio interview from my office at my day job while finishing up a motion that had to be filed with the court," explains Riviere.

Currently, she is working with a local network television station to develop content for a morning talk show. "It is hard to find time for public relations with a fulltime job, the blog, styling, and life!" she says.

Riviere would love for her creative business to be a full-time thing, but says she is fine if that never happens. "I am trying to let everything evolve organically and never push myself too hard because I don't want to take the fun away from it," she notes.

She says she wants to make time for her personal life in addition to her full-time job and creative gig. "If I am going to enjoy my life and earn a comfortable living, I have to accept that everything is not going to happen overnight," says Riviere.

At the time this book was published, Riviere was happy to report that she is no longer at her law job and now manages the blog and is a freelance fashion consultant. While her transition didn't happen overnight, she did wind up shifting into life as a full-time freelancer. (But I kept her story in because it's just that inspiring!)"

 I was offered a contract gig that could go full-time. It seems like a good opportunity, but I don't want my freelance clients to suffer. How can I keep the balance?

"First thing to do is to explain to your freelance clients you are no longer available to work during normal working hours. This might

not work with every client or type of profession, but it is important they know so they have time to adjust to the situation. Many projects I've done tend to have a range of deadlines from immediate to a few weeks. So some projects are possible to work on during your off hours and/or on the weekend, while others are not doable."

—Tim Goldman, illustrator/designer,
www.timgoldman.com

Basking in the Moonlight

Not everyone wants their creative business to become a full-time thing. In fact, several successful businesses hatch by people that work full-time jobs and run their enterprise on the side with no intention for that to change.

Sarah Griffin hopes to continue working full-time as a chemist and have a flourishing creative business on the side; she doesn't plan on quitting her traditional job. She started the Web site *www.secretsivenevertold.com* and wound up writing a book, *Secrets I Never Told,* as a way to keep the right side of her brain active and give people a way to communicate their pent-up secrets anonymously.

The 20-something Kansas resident says most of her work is done before or after business hours, so it usually doesn't interfere with her work. "Every day I wake up around 5 a.m. to update the Web site and check e-mail before I leave for work," says Griffin. "Often I'll have interviews during normal business hours, and in that case I'll take an hour or two of paid time off and go back to work after the interview."

At first, all the work put a huge dent in her social life, but as time has gone on, she is learning to manage it better. "Owning your own business means that there is constantly something to do and always something to improve on," notes Griffin. That is the kind of attitude that I think separates successful freelancers from those that are not so effective.

By keeping her full-time job and the stability it offers, it takes some of the burden off Griffin to excel quickly at her secondary profession. That said, it doesn't mean she works any less on it or that it is any less successful than a full-time creative business. Moonlighting is what you put into it, and, as Griffin has learned, it takes time to settle in no matter what type of creative business you have.

She recently secured a few television and radio spots to promote her business and draws profits from her book sales—all while mixing things up in a lab by day.

How have you mentally overcome frustration with your in-flux status between holding down a full-time job and freelancing?

"Many designers take great pride in coming home to a night shift of personal or outside projects; I've always hated the extra workload. Both the daytime gigs (working on-site in a multi-week temporary job) and the after-hours work (my own clients and a variety of smaller, independent projects) have been unpredictable. Arrange your personal time so that you can dedicate more time to work. Cancel your dinner plans, push the laundry to next week, and accept that you won't be going to the gym. Remember finals week in college? It's basically that. The good news is that it's temporary. If you're continually running yourself ragged doing outside work, something has to give. Perhaps you finally have enough work to go full-time freelance."

—Prescott Perez-Fox, art director/graphic designer,
www.strshp.com

Taking the Nosedive: Going Full-Time With Your Creative Biz

For some people, having a side business is the ultimate goal, but what if you want more? Say you've been freelancing for a few months or years, and you would rather pursue your freelance business. How do you get there? It's not as easy as "Dive in! The water's great!" There are practical things to consider, such as meeting your financial obligations without a guaranteed paycheck. The whole "plunge" into full-time freelancing concept can feel more like a polar bear plunge instead of a scuba dive.

Before oregon-based illustrative designer Von Glitschka (*www. vonglitschka.com*) started his successful career, he worked in the communications arena. Glitschka moonlighted since he got out of school, but the thought of making a full-time business out of his freelance status was hard; he had a wife and two children to support. "What held me back was just fear of the unknown," confesses Glitschka.

When he was fired from his job as an art director and he couldn't find another position, his wife told him to start the creative business he had always dreamed of. Glitschka experienced the typical trial-and-error years, but eventually got his footing and is now making a gratifying living off his talents.

Angela Ferraro-Fanning (*www.1331design.com*) from New Jersey took a different route to attain her goal of managing her own graphic design business. She'd always been in the design industry, but her full-time job as an art director at the time wouldn't allow her to work part-time for her own clients. So she quit cold turkey, took a part-time gig at a candy store, and pursued her freelance endeavor.

"I wanted something mindless where I could show up for work and leave it there when my shift was done," recalls Ferraro-Fanning, who has been self-employed since 2005. "Every day, I woke up early and started my day with my own business no later than 7 a.m. I worked until noon and then headed to the candy store until 5 p.m.," she says. Although some of her coworkers were high school students, and some of her customers were also clients, the humbling experience helped her get her business off the ground. Within just two months of starting work at the candy store, she was able to take her business full-time and sustain it.

This is a pretty neat approach if you want to take the plunge because it enables you to make money while giving your creative side a rest. Then you are raring to go and work on your business when your shift is over, much like I was when I moonlighted. The financial safety net, regardless of whether it comes from a well-paying professional role or a minimum wage job, can make all the difference as you transition from a moonlighter into a business owner.

When did you know it was right to go solo?

"I don't think you ever know for sure the time is right. I was scared to make the jump, but it was convenient timing and I had been very busy with freelance work. My husband and I determined how much I would need to make to be able to freelance full time and not get a part-time job, and I have hit that minimum ever since."

—April Michelle Davis, editor/indexer/proofreader,
www.editorialinspirations.com

Taking the Next Step

My plunge, described in Chapter 1, was less of a dive and more like wading. I was very practical about transitioning into a full-time free-lance role and took my time doing so, primarily motivated by a fear of being penniless.

So was Grace Smith (*www.postscript5.co.uk*), a Web designer based in Ireland, who moonlighted for about six months while she worked in a local print shop. For her, juggling both acts became a huge challenge, so moving to a full-time format was the next logical step. She had a roster of clients and plenty of work, which helped her segue into life as a full-time freelancer. "It reaches a stage where freelancing full-time is the natural progression," she notes. A lot of fellow full-time free-lancers I hear from have found that when they got too busy and were working 70- and 80-hour weeks—and sustaining that momentum over time—they knew it was time to seriously consider shifting to a full-time self-employment role.

Even though you get super-busy, how do you know when you can hurdle from moonlighter to business owner? You may be swamped with work but still unable financially to "go freelance." It takes time for those who are rooted in practicality—or fear! Still, others that quit their jobs cold turkey and launched their businesses have also been quite successful. It really depends on the person.

Even though I do not have children to support, I was very anxious when I thought about going solo because I had rent and bills to pay. Being self-employed would mean paying for my own health insurance as well—how frightening! Through time, as I cultivated more credibility and more projects came in, I saw that the business was becoming sustainable. That was, I figured, the best possible place to be when I took the plunge. All I had to do was get out of my own way, look fear square in its face, and go for it.

How do you approach your boss at either a temporary or permanent full-time job about your freelance work?

"As long as you're not competing with your employer, it's usually a non-issue. But if your side gig is steadily becoming your main focus, you should be open with your boss. Tell him or her how much you love working there, but that you also love working on the side gig. Much like a new parent asking to leave 'early' at 5:00 p.m., you're making the visible efforts to be balanced and not to neglect either role. A reasonable boss will understand. If anything, he'll see that the new creative energy benefits the organization when you're back in the next day."

—Prescott Perez-Fox, art director/graphic designer,
www.strshp.com

Smith went through a similar experience. She built up three months' worth of her salary prior to starting as a full-time freelancer. "Having this security would mean I could focus purely on client work, growing connections and networking, without the initial pressure of creating an income from the first month," recalls Smith.

Some people believe that a few months' worth of savings will do it, but I contend that proving your business is stable is a more reliable method. To test the waters, see if you really like being a contractor first. Obviously if you are married, your decision affects others, so you'll want to discuss the matter with your family as well.

In Smith's case, it wasn't just about money. What really helped her leap was having confidence in her abilities. This stemmed from working in the art and design field for many years before launching her solo biz. She knew she had talent and that, with her drive, she could turn her natural gifts into profits. "Being able to express your thoughts and ideas is half the battle; having confidence in what you are saying is the other half," she says.

Putting thought into the plunging process was important for Smith, who does not think anyone is ever 100-percent ready to become a full-time freelancer. You can have a decent nest egg saved up and all the clients in the world, but until you see that you can keep the cash—and the clients—coming in, it may be hard to feel comfortable leaving a cushy full-time job...even one you can't stand. This is precisely why moonlighting works so well: You can demonstrate to yourself through time that the business is functioning well, which makes it much easier to surge to the next level.

"The key is to know ahead of time what being ready means," says Smith, noting that being ready means different things to everyone. "That way, when the moment comes, you can take the emotion out of it and make a decision based on facts."

Freelancing full-time was a natural evolution for Ed Gandia (*www. edgandia.com*), a copywriter from Georgia who also co-founded International Freelancer's Day (*www.internationalfreelancersday.com*). He worked in sales and account management, and then moonlighted for more than two years before launching his copywriting business about seven years ago. He decided to leverage his sales background into copywriting, and credits classes at the American Writers & Artists Institute (AWAI) to help him learn the art of copywriting. "I'm wired to make my own decisions," he says of its innate ability to run his own business.

A majority of solo-pros who start a creative business—whether as moonlighters or full-timers—cite wanting to be their own boss as a major reason to launch their venture. I don't think anyone likes having a boss, but some people have a higher tolerance for working under someone else. Even if you have a wonderful superior, you still may not like being under the supervision of others in general. When I worked for other companies, I enjoyed enhancing my capabilities but I wanted to have more of a say in things.

April Michelle Davis (*www.editorialinspirations.com*), a freelance editor, indexer, and proofreader from Virginia, never intended to be her own boss. She toyed with the idea of starting her own business but says she moonlighted for six years because she was too afraid to jump into full-time freelancing. In that time, she didn't just wait for customers to come in—she worked her butt off to create a Web site and build a name for herself before she saw that she had a solid and regenerating clientele base. When she knew that she had the ability to create new opportunities for herself on an ongoing basis, she felt more comfortable shifting into life as a solo-pro.

Upon graduating with her master's degree in publishing, she and her husband were in the midst of relocating. Together, they decided she could quit her job and freelance full-time as long as she brought in a certain amount of money, taking on a part-time job if she needed it. She has been blissfully busy ever since, and never needed to take another job.

Must-Read
Grow Your Handmade Business: How to Envision, Develop, and Sustain a Successful Creative Business **by Kari Chapin**

Moonlighters Have to Follow the Rules, Too

Part of running a legitimate and successful business has to do with money, as you have read throughout the book. Even if you are moonlighting and you don't ever want to turn your side biz into a full-time career, finances come into play. For many, it is what dictates whether or not they can leave their traditional job to pursue life as a full-time solo-pro.

Another financial aspect of moonlighting includes taxes. That's right, even if you have a traditional job, you still have to pay taxes on what you earn from your side business. Just as you would if you were self-employed, talk to an accountant to cover specifics on setting up your business, establishing money management practices, and filing taxes as a moonlighter.

Not only do you have to manage your money; incorporating good legal business practices is just as important as is it to market your business and develop client relationships. To have a solid business, you want to make sure you play by professional standards.

What are some of the differences when paying taxes as a moonlighter as opposed to a full-time solo professional?

"There is no real difference in your responsibility for paying taxes or in your ability to take deductions. Any income you earn as a freelancer—an unincorporated entity—will be subject to self-employment tax, no matter the hours worked. Where it will make a difference, however, is in how you plan to pay the additional taxes from your moonlighting. Moonlighting implies you have another, perhaps full-time, gig as an employee. If that is the case you can adjust your W-2 or employee withholdings to cover the moonlighting liability or you can pay estimated taxes in addition to your normal withholdings. The IRS does not care which pocket you pay the taxes from—it is all part of your individual tax liability."

—Richard Streitfeld, accountant,
www.peaceloveandbusinessplanning.com

Now What?

Regardless of the type of business you want or have, it's important to be practical and professional. Blending your creative talents and business know-how is your best recipe for success. Remember that it's okay to feel things out as you go. It is good to test the waters and try approaches that will work for you. So long as you play by a few rules, your business is uniquely yours to manage. Hopefully this book is a resource you can count on as you go.

That's the beauty in owning a book chock full of business advice for creative professionals; now you have all the tools you need to flourish.

Sweet Success
Back-and-Forth Freelancing

Jane Hodges (*www.janehodges.net*) bounced back and forth between staff writing positions and freelance roles over the past 20 years. Even when she worked on staff at publications such as *Ad Age,* she always moonlighted on the side.

"I always had an idea that I wanted to be a freelance writer, ever since I was a kid. I'd save my allowance, ride to the drug store, and load up on magazines," recalls Hodges, who currently resides in Seattle. Hodges thought she would need to be on a magazine's staff until she was in her mid-30s to break into freelance writing on a full-time basis, but had the opportunity to start freelancing full-time when she left a traditional full-time role at the age of 29. (Hodges did return to a traditional full-time job in 2002 when she relocated from New York to Seattle, but left that job in 2004 and has been a full-time solo-pro ever since.)

Hodges has written articles on a freelance basis for *The Wall Street Journal, The New York Times, AOL HousingWatch, Fortune, Entrepreneur.com*, and *Newsday,* just to name a few. She says that she has always had one or more steady paying gigs, which she says are almost like permanent part-time jobs. "I feel like, with the kind of economy we have, everything is, ultimately, a 'gig'— even a full-time job," says Hodges, who recently published another book.

Beginner Mishap
A Pressing Matter

One of the things many freelancers strive to do is drum up business for themselves—and a great way to do that is to secure coverage in the media. Is all press good press, though?

Lori Riviere knows firsthand that a media mention isn't always a plus. The Miami-based fashion blogger and stylist is always open to getting coverage in order to promote her Web site, *www.shortcutsto-fabulous.com.*

She got the opportunity to have an interview with a CNN reporter, and claims the journalist said she was going to be featuring Riviere's blog as a part of a story on middle-class Americans dining out less to save money for luxury goods. Ideally, that would be good—especially if her Web site wound up getting more traffic from the article.

However, Riviere says she was misled. She claims the article did not focus on the topic she was originally told about, and she says her quotes were pulled out of context. "Not only did she [the CNN reporter] not feature my blog, she mischaracterized my statements and made me sound awful for a story whose headline was 'Rich Americans Flock to Fast Food,'" she explains. "The story did not fit in with the brand image I am trying to create for myself and Shortcuts to Fabulous."

Although the Web site wasn't included in the story, the piece still affected her. She worked a day job as a lawyer at the time, and said several colleagues teased her about the article. "It was a rather humiliating lesson that I shouldn't have had to learn...but I am glad I learned it early," she admits.

Afterword

In writing this book, I have tried to provide you with the foundation needed to build a thriving business. Instead of providing well-calculated formulas and methods, I chose to share the basics and let you glean ideas from others who have been in your shoes. They brought up different approaches that you can collect insight from. Some will work; some won't. If I've really accomplished my mission in writing this book, your creative juices will start flowing and you'll come up with your own ideas. You'll carve your own path. Creatives are individuals.

As I've mentioned, growing your business requires you to use your judgment and common sense to determine which practices are best for you. That's the magic of being self-employed: *You* get to make the rules. Work in your undies, take three-day weekends, hand-pick clients—it's all *you.*

Refer back to this book as you develop your talents *and* your business. Through time, you will find that the two seem to fuse naturally. That is, you will expand your natural gifts and you will grow adept in running a business.

You may never want to deal with some parts of being a solo-pro, but when you start to activate your inner businessperson, you'll be able to manage every aspect of your business. It is going to feel good to be on top of everything—not just your talent. In growing this business—this part of yourself—the rewards will be endless.

Resources

Websites

Creativity and Freelancing

www.creativebusiness.com
www.creativelatitude.com
www.creativesuccess.com
www.entrepreneur.com
www.fastcompany.com
www.forgraphicdesignersonly.com
www.freelanceradio.com
www.freelanceswitch.com
www.freelanceunleashed.com
www.howdesign.com
www.internationalfreelancersday.com
www.marketingmixblog.com
www.mediabistro.com
www.rightbrainbusinessplan.com
www.smartcreativewomen.com
www.smashingmagazine.com
www.thecreativecareer.com
www.theswitchboards.com

Finding Work

www.aquent.com

www.behance.net

www.bloggingpro.com

www.craigslist.com

www.creativecircle.com

www.creativehotlist.com

www.creativegroup.com

www.freelancesuccess.com

www.freelancewriting.com

www.freelancewritingjobs.com

www.flexjobs.com

www.krop.com

www.peopleperhour.com

www.talentzoo.com

www.writersweekly.com

Legal Resources

www.creativecommons.org

www.findlaw.com

www.lawdepot.com

www.legalzoom.com

www.license123.com

www.legalmatch.com

www.nolo.com

www.sba.gov

Marketing and Social Networking

www.agencyaccess.com

www.allgraphicdesign.com

www.creativeaccess.com

www.helpareporter.com

www.langermanlists.com
www.linkedin.com
www.facebook.com
www.twitter.com
www.marketing-mentor.com
www.marketingprofs.com
www.prnewswire.com
www.prweb.com
www.thelistinc.com

Accounting and Bookkeeping

www.blinksale.com
www.cashboardapp.com
www.freshbooks.com
www.getcashboard.com
www.getharvest.com
www.invoicemachine.com
www.lessaccounting.com
www.moneycrashers.com
www.outright.com
www.paypal.com
www.quickbooks.intuit.com
www.simplyinvoices.com
www.stripe.com

Productivity and Tools

www.basecamp.com
www.creattica.com
www.conceptshare.com
www.dropbox.com
www.getklok.com
www.gotomeeting.com
www.mozy.com

www.mycpohq.com

www.openoffice.org

www.rememberthemilk.com

Education

www.aionline.edu

www.communication-central.com

www.internationalfreelancersacademy.com

www.lynda.com

www.freelancersu.com

www.freelanceworkshops.com

www.worldwidelearn.com

Organizations, Certifications, and Conferences

Adobe Certified Experts—*www.adobe.com/support/certification/ace.html*

AIGA—*www.aiga.org*

American Society of Journalists and Authors—*www.asja.org*

BlogHer—*www.blogher.com*

Design Management Institute—*www.dmi.org*

Editorial Freelancers Association—*www.the-efa.org*

Freelancers Union—*www.freelancersunion.org*

Graphic Artists Guild—*www.graphicartistsguild.org*

HOW Design Live/Creative Freelancer Conference—*www.how-designlive.com*

International Freelancers Academy—*www.internationalfreelancer-sacademy.com*

MediaBistro Copy Editing Certification—*www.mediabistro.com*

Microsoft Certifications—*www.microsoft.com/learning*

New Media Expo—*www.blogworldexpo.com*

Push Workshops—*www.pushworkshops.com*

Society of Professional Journalists—*www.spj.org*

South by Southwest—*www.sxsw.com*

99u Conference—*www.99u.com*

Index

About the Author

Kristen Fischer is a copywriter and journalist who has been self-employed for more than seven years. She has written articles for *Writer's Digest, New Jersey Monthly, HOW Magazine,* and *MediaBistro.com,* and is a panelist on Freelance Radio. Kristen is a Certified Professional Resume Writer.

She is a graduate of the Richard Stockton College of New Jersey. Kristen lives at the Jersey Shore with her husband and three cats: Hope, Brady, and Skeeter. Learn more about her at *www.kristenfischer.com.*